Can Democracy Handle
Climate Change?

T0273740

Democratic Futures series

Stephen Coleman, *Can the Internet Strengthen Democracy?*
Drude Dahlerup, *Has Democracy Failed Women?*
Donald F. Kettl, *Can Governments Earn Our Trust?*
Alasdair Roberts, *Can Government Do Anything Right?*

Daniel J. Fiorino

———

Can Democracy Handle Climate Change?

Polity

Copyright © Daniel J. Fiorino 2018

The right of Daniel J. Fiorino to be identified as Author of this Work has been asserted in accordance with the UK Copyright, Designs and Patents Act 1988.

First published in 2018 by Polity Press

Polity Press
65 Bridge Street
Cambridge CB2 1UR, UK

Polity Press
101 Station Landing
Suite 300
Medford, MA 02155, USA

All rights reserved. Except for the quotation of short passages for the purpose of criticism and review, no part of this publication may be reproduced, stored in a retrieval system or transmitted, in any form or by any means, electronic, mechanical, photocopying, recording or otherwise, without the prior permission of the publisher.

ISBN-13: 978-1-5095-2395-5
ISBN-13: 978-1-5095-2396-2(pb)

A catalogue record for this book is available from the British Library.

Typeset in 11 on 15pt Sabon
by Fakenham Prepress Solutions, Fakenham, Norfolk NR21 8NN

The publisher has used its best endeavours to ensure that the URLs for external websites referred to in this book are correct and active at the time of going to press. However, the publisher has no responsibility for the websites and can make no guarantee that a site will remain live or that the content is or will remain appropriate.

Every effort has been made to trace all copyright holders, but if any have been inadvertently overlooked the publisher will be pleased to include any necessary credits in any subsequent reprint or edition.

For further information on Polity, visit our website:
politybooks.com

Contents

Tables

Preface

The end of 2017 brought reports that the extent and impacts of climate change could be far worse than previous scenarios had suggested. A study published in the *Proceedings of the National Academy of Sciences* in the United States concluded there is a one in twenty chance that the world could experience "catastrophic" warming between 2050 and 2100, enough to pose an "existential" threat to global populations.[1]

The next month, the World Meteorological Organization's Global Atmosphere Watch determined that atmospheric concentrations of greenhouse gases had reached their highest level in 800,000 years. Rapidly increasing concentrations of greenhouse gases, the WMO Greenhouse Gas Bulletin found, "have the potential to initiate unpredictable changes in the climate system ...

leading to severe ecological and economic disruptions."[2] A week later, an updated National Climate Assessment in the United States issued what the *Washington Post* termed a "dire" report that warns of "a worst-case scenario where seas would rise as high as eight feet by the year 2100, and details climate-related damage across the United States that is already unfolding as a result of an average global temperature increase of 1.8 degrees Fahrenheit since 1900."[3]

All of this came on top of years of accumulating evidence on the severity of the threats posed by climate change and its ecological, health, economic, social, and political impacts. These threats, most of them concentrated on the poorest and most vulnerable of the world's population, have created doubts about the ability of governments around the world to cope with the causes and impacts of climate change. Democracies in particular have been the object of skepticism. Confronting the existential and catastrophic threat of a changing climate is, many critics argue, akin to fighting a major war. Whether democracy is able to effectively take up the challenge of mitigating and adapting to climate change will determine what kind of planet we pass on to future generations.

Acknowledgments

This book considers the interrelationships and inter-dependencies between two of the big issues of our time. One is climate change, often described as the greatest governance challenge of this century. The other is the quality and durability of democracy, the benefits of which are substantial but whose capacities for handling climate mitigation and adaptation have been doubted.

Thanks first go to Louise Knight at Polity Press, who encouraged me to explore this topic and offered support and guidance throughout the process. Thanks also to Nekane Tanaka Galdos at Polity for help at many points along the way and to Tim Clark for his careful copy-editing.

I also want to acknowledge the reviewers for Polity, who were thorough, thoughtful, and offered valuable advice. Special thanks for taking the time

Acknowledgments

to review the manuscript and offer many valuable suggestions go to Jonathan Boston of Victoria University in New Zealand and to Robert Durant and Paul Bledsoe of American University in the United States. Thanks also to American University students Mikayla Pellerin and David Peters for their research assistance.

I am indebted to my wife Beth Ann for her encouragement and support, and to Matthew and Jacob, whose interest and stake in the future of both the climate and democracy are compelling.

1

The Challenge to Governance

Can democracy handle climate change? Some experts think not. According to the distinguished scientist and founder of the Gaia theory, James Lovelock, "Even the best democracies agree that when a major war approaches, democracy must be put on hold for the time being. I have a feeling that climate change may be an issue as severe as a war. It may be necessary to put democracy on hold for a while."[1] The problem with democracies, so the argument goes, is that they are crippled by inertia, dominated by vested interests, and incapable of responding to existential risks such as climate change.

For Lovelock and other skeptics, democracies cannot make the hard choices needed to avoid the worst impacts of a changing climate for the rest of this century and beyond. They rely too much on the consent of a public that puts short-term gratification over long-term well-being. Democracies must respect individual rights and follow procedures that are unlikely to deliver the actions required within the necessary time frame. Voters lack the scientific knowledge needed to grasp the causes of climate change and its multiple threats to humans and the planet. Democracies are too slow, materialistic, and sclerotic to meet the complex challenges involved.

In contrast, the skeptics argue, authoritarian regimes are better able to impose solutions from the top down, no matter how unpleasant they may be in the short term. They can overcome opposition from powerful interests in fossil fuels, agriculture, land development, and elsewhere in order to enforce reductions in emissions and changes in economic and social systems. Unlike democratic regimes, they are free to implement the proposals of experts who grasp the complexities of climate science, and can override popular desires for ever-increasing consumption and immediate material gratification to achieve what is best for citizens and the planet in the long run.

This skepticism is reflected in public views in many parts of the world, even in the more established and successful democracies. Economic uncertainty, rising economic inequality, mass immigration, and changes resulting from globalization have led many citizens to doubt the value of democracy. Drawing upon data from the World Values Survey, Roberto Foa and Yascha Mounk highlight this broad dissatisfaction with democratic institutions and values. In France, for example, two-fifths of respondents in 2016 thought the country should be run by an authoritarian government, while two-thirds thought authority for "unpopular but necessary reforms" should be handed over to "unelected experts." Likewise, in the United States, the proportion supporting military rule rose from one in sixteen in 1995 to one in six in 2016. There is a generational aspect to these findings: 72 percent of Americans born before World War II say that living in a democracy is "essential"; for post-1980 millennials the comparable response is 30 percent.[2] Similar trends are apparent in other countries.

The skeptics' case has certainly gained currency given recent events in the United States and China, the two largest economies, and greenhouse gas emitters, in the world. Yet it is authoritarian China, not the democratic United States, that is often perceived to be moving to address climate change. It is on a path to stabilizing emissions ahead of the schedule it committed to in the 2015 Paris Agreement on climate change, and is making major investments in renewable energy technologies – twice the US levels in 2016.

In contrast, although US emissions fell some 10 percent between 2005 and 2014, and several climate mitigation initiatives were introduced under President Barack Obama, this course was rapidly reversed at the national level following the election of Donald Trump. President Trump announced his intent to withdraw from the Paris Agreement; to reverse regulations designed to reduce emissions, including the critically important Clean Power Plan; to drastically cut renewable energy and efficiency funding; and to undo strict vehicle fuel economy standards.[3]

This chapter introduces the problem of climate change and the challenges it poses to governance. As Ross Garnaut wrote in a report for the Australian government in 2011: "Climate change is like no other environmental problem that humanity has ever faced ... the failure of our generation [to address it] would lead to consequences that would haunt humanity to the end of time."[4]

What is climate change?

One reason given for doubting democracy's ability to address the problem adequately is that global efforts to reduce greenhouse gas emissions and manage the other causes of climate change have been, to this point, insufficient to avoid many of its worst impacts. Based on the assessments of the Intergovernmental Panel on Climate Change (IPCC) and other scientific bodies, atmospheric concentrations of greenhouse gases would have to level off at some 450–550 parts per million by 2050.[5] Yet, far from meeting this target, the world is on a path of increasing emissions and land-use changes that will only add to the problem.[6]

The United Nations defines the issue as "a change of climate which is attributed directly or indirectly to human activity that alters the composition of the global atmosphere and which is in addition to natural climate vulnerability observed over comparable time periods."[7] The key here is the link to human activity and its role in contributing to abnormal variations that have profound effects. The most recent report of the US Global Change Research Program, for example, concluded "that it is extremely likely that human activities, especially emissions of greenhouse gases, are the dominant cause of the observed warming since the mid-20th century."[8]

For our purposes, climate change refers to the increase in global average temperatures that has occurred over roughly the past half-century and to the ecological effects of this increase. The primary cause is the growing concentrations of greenhouse gases in the atmosphere, related mostly but not entirely to fossil fuel combustion. The main gases involved are carbon dioxide, methane, nitrous oxide, and fluorinated gases. In its 2014 assessment, the IPCC reported that in 2010 carbon dioxide from fossil fuel use and industrial processes accounted for some 65 percent of total greenhouse gases, followed by carbon dioxide from changes in forestry and land use (11 percent), methane (at 16 percent), nitrous oxide (just over 6 percent), and fluorinated gases (2 percent). The pace of emissions has grown in recent decades: one-half of human-caused emissions since 1750 occurred in the last forty years.[9] These gases also have different effects in their warming potential. Carbon dioxide stays in the atmosphere for hundreds or thousands of years, while others are shorter-lived but have larger warming effects. Table 1.1 describes the gases and their respective warming potential.

Until just a few decades ago, most emissions came from the developed world: the United States, Europe, Japan, and so on. More recently, rapid economic growth has led to higher emissions from China, India and other parts of Asia, Latin America,

The Challenge to Governance

Table 1.1: Main Greenhouse Gases and their Global Warming Potential (GWP)

Gas	Main sources	Percentage of global emissions	GWP
Carbon dioxide	Fossil fuels & industrial processes	65 percent	1.0 (= the standard for stating the effects of other gases in terms of CO_2 equivalents)
	Forestry & land use	11 percent	
Methane	Agricultural activity Waste management (e.g. landfills) Biomass burning	16 percent	28–32 times that of CO_2 over a 100-year period
Nitrous oxide	Agriculture (e.g. fertilizer) Fossil fuels	6 percent	265–98 times that of CO_2 over 100-year period
Fluorinated gases	Refrigeration Industrial/consumer uses	2 percent	Thousands to tens of thousands of times that of CO_2 but over short time periods

Source: US Environmental Protection Agency (IPCC emissions data from 2010)[10]

and parts of Africa. In 2010, 42 percent of emissions were from countries in the Organization for Economic Cooperation and Development (OECD, a group of thirty-five more affluent countries), and 58 percent from non-OECD countries; by 2040 they are projected to be 32 percent OECD and 68 percent non-OECD.[11]

These totals disguise variation in emissions per capita and per dollar of Gross Domestic Product. According to the World Bank, per capita US carbon dioxide emissions in 2014 were 16.5 and China's 7.5 metric tons. In contrast, countries like India, Vietnam, and Morocco were below two tons annually.[12] In carbon intensity (emissions per unit of income), countries like the Russian Federation and China were less efficient than the United States and the European Union. In brief, the early industrializers were the dominant emitters in the last century, and until recently contributed the most to the concentration of atmospheric greenhouse gases. The newer high-growth economies with large populations will dominate future emissions. Both need to reduce their emissions substantially if we are to avoid the worst impacts of a changing climate.

Although greenhouse gas emissions are the major source of climate change, land use and forestry practices also play a prominent role. Deforestation contributes to the problem because trees and other vegetation absorb carbon and act as an emissions sink. Agricultural practices also affect the amount of carbon stored in soil. This is why forest protection, reforestation, afforestation, and conservation agriculture are major elements in the strategy to combat climate change. Land use can also support adaptation efforts by offsetting the effects of warming at local levels, such as through tree planting and green infrastructure projects.[13]

The impacts of climate change

The problem with a changing climate is not only increasing global average temperatures but the rate of change and the impacts rising temperatures have on natural and human systems. Global and regional climates have always changed; the issue now is that human activity is forcing more rapid and disruptive modifications in global climate that lead to harmful impacts. As noted in the preface, atmospheric concentrations of greenhouse gases are now the highest they have been in 800,000 years. The average global temperature is one degree Celsius above pre-industrial levels, and is rising at an increasing rate.

Can Democracy Handle Climate Change?

Among the impacts are rising sea levels, changes in precipitation, melting glaciers, more extreme weather events like hurricanes, crop losses, disruption to terrestrial and aquatic ecosystems, human health risks, food insecurity and the breakdown of food systems, and higher levels of droughts and flooding. There will be more coastal flooding, a loss of critical infrastructure (e.g. the electrical grid or the water supply), political instability and an increase in refugees, death and illness from extreme heat, and water shortages and stresses. The issue is not just the warming but the disruption it will cause to a range of natural and social systems.

A major part of the challenge is the uncertainty: although the climate is changing due to human activity, the pace of change and the extent of its impacts are hard to predict. A major source of that uncertainty is evidenced in two phenomena: positive feedback loops and tipping points. The first refers to how the impacts of climate change can also reinforce it; for example, a melting of permafrost in northern latitudes will increase carbon emissions. Tipping points are "thresholds for abrupt change" which increase the risk of worst-case predictions being realized.[14] Reinforcing this, many such effects are irreversible: once a threshold is breached there is no going back.

The Challenge to Governance

Of course, a changing climate is not the only source of environmental stress. Economic and population growth, industrialization, urbanization, fossil fuel use, water consumption, land use, and other trends since World War II have fueled large-scale worries about the health of the planet and human well-being. The rise of the modern environmental movement in the 1960s and 1970s responded to these trends. Climate change adds not only a new set of threats but a force that magnifies and interacts with existing threats. Hotter weather intensifies the effects of air pollution on health; droughts exacerbate problems of water availability; sea-level rises threaten coastal estuaries; crop and productivity losses undermine adaptation capacities – the list goes on.

At the same time, however, the need to deal with the causes of climate change creates opportunities. Moving from fossil fuels to renewables and from internal combustion engines to electrified vehicles greatly reduces air pollution. Innovation in the water sector not only conserves and better allocates water resources but also saves energy and enhances water quality and availability. Restoring carbon sinks through forest protection and reforestation protects habitat and livelihoods. These opportunities also extend to the economy, having beneficial effects in terms of energy conservation, improved health and productivity, smarter land use, and new investment and job options.

International agreements on climate change

The problems of climate change will not be solved by a single country or even a group of countries. Greenhouse gas emissions anywhere add to climate change everywhere. Addressing the causes calls for collective international action. The first major climate agreement was negotiated at the Rio Earth Summit in 1992, in the form of the United Nations Framework Convention on Climate Change (UNFCCC). This did not involve commitments or specific actions; its purpose was to set out a process as well as establish principles and goals for negotiating more specific agreements.[15]

Article 2 of the UNFCCC set a goal that has guided climate change mitigation negotiations from the start: the "stabilization of greenhouse gas concentrations in the atmosphere at a level that would prevent dangerous anthropogenic interference with the climate system."[16] The IPCC works on the assumption that atmospheric concentrations of greenhouse gases should be held to a range of

450–550 parts per million (ppm) by 2050 to avoid the worst impacts of climate change.

The first international climate agreement to include commitments was the Kyoto Protocol, signed in 1997 and later ratified by 191 countries, although not by the United States. The overall goal was to cut global emissions to 5 percent below 1990 levels by 2012. The commitments varied: 8 percent for the European Union, 6 percent for Canada, and 7 percent for the United States – had it participated. Developing countries, including China and India, were exempt. Although global emissions grew by nearly 40 percent from 1990 to 2009, this was 29 percent below what would have occurred under the likely "business as usual" scenario.

Easily the most significant step forward came at the Paris Conference of the Parties in December 2015. At the heart of the agreement were the "intended nationally determined commitments" (INDCs) from over 180 countries, with self-defined mitigation goals, starting in 2020. Both the United States and China submitted INDCs that built on a bilateral agreement reached in November 2015: the US committed to a 26–28 percent cut from its 2005 emission levels by 2025; China would level emissions and generate at least 20 percent of electricity from renewables, both by 2025. The agreement entered into force in October 2016 with 169 of the 197 Parties to the Convention having ratified it.[17]

The Paris Agreement reaffirmed the goal of limiting average temperature increases to two degrees Celsius by mid-century, but set an "aspirational" goal of limiting it to 1.5 degrees.[18] In reality, it is estimated that if all the INDCs are implemented there will still be a roughly 2.7 degree increase by 2100, although this is far better than the predicted 3.6 degree rise without the INDCs.[19] There is reason for both pessimism and optimism in such numbers. Countries may not meet all their commitments, but once change is underway it may proceed faster than was anticipated.

A productive follow-up to the Paris conference was another agreement reached in Kigali, Rwanda in 2016. The Kigali Amendment to the Montreal Protocol (an earlier agreement on chemicals that deplete stratospheric ozone) set the terms for a phase-out of hydrofluorocarbons, a class of chemicals with thousands of times the greenhouse gas effects of carbon dioxide. It is expected to reduce average global temperatures in the range of 0.5 or more degrees Celsius if fully implemented by 2100.[20]

The Challenge to Governance

Mitigation and adaptation

Climate change presents the world with two kinds of challenges – mitigation and adaptation. The IPCC defines mitigation as "a human intervention to reduce the sources or enhance the sinks of greenhouse gases."[21] The challenge is to change energy, transportation, water, agriculture, manufacturing, and other systems to reduce the flow of greenhouse gases into the atmosphere and expand the available sinks through forestry and land-use practices. Yet many of the consequences of climate change are already apparent, and others are inevitable given current projections and insufficient mitigation. The second challenge is adaptation, which is the "process of adjustment to actual or expected climate and its effects."[22] This means having the ability to avoid or moderate the adverse impacts of change.

This book focuses on the ability of democracies to handle the mitigation challenge, because this is where skeptics have raised most of their doubts and where most of the research has been conducted. Furthermore, systematic action to develop capacities for adapting to climate change is far more recent, and there is less of a track record to examine. Still, in the final chapter, I consider how

15

democracies and other regimes may be able to address the adaptation challenge.

Before moving on, it will be helpful to clarify two of the terms used throughout the book: *Climate action* describes the policies, investments, technologies, and behavior changes that are aimed at managing the emission sources and land-use changes principally behind climate change. *Governance* refers to the ways in which societies organize themselves for the purposes of managing conflict and achieving their goals; it is broader in scope and incorporates a wider range of actors than does the term *government*.

Defining democracy

As a form of governance, democracy is usually distinguished from other forms by a set of core characteristics: free and fair elections, majority rule by representative institutions, limits on governmental power, and protection of individual and minority rights. Authority ultimately rests on the consent of the governed rather than on the preferences of some set of elites. In their institutional characteristics, democracies typically operate on the basis of a fundamental law in the form of a constitution, with an independent judiciary, distinctions among legislative and executive authorities, and political freedoms.[23]

For my purposes, a useful source for defining and measuring democracy is the Economist Intelligence Unit's (EIU) Democracy Index. This incorporates measures of political freedom and civil liberty, which are seen as central to any definition of democracy. However, these measures taken on their own are "thin," and tend to miss less tangible yet still substantive aspects of democracy. The EIU approach aims for a "thicker" definition with measures reflecting political participation, political culture, and the functioning of government. The EIU Democracy Index provides a thorough, accessible, and regularly updated set of measures for comparing national political systems.[24]

The Index includes assessments in five categories: electoral process and pluralism, civil liberties, the functioning of government, political participation, and political culture. For each there are indicators for placing systems on a numerical scale. In addition to the five categories, the Index incorporates four overarching measures: free and fair elections, security in voting, foreign influence on government, and capacity of the civil service to implement public policies.

Using this method, each of 167 countries is given a score from 1 to 10 and placed in one of four groups. *Full democracies* (nineteen countries) meet the standard criteria on elections, political freedom, and civil liberty, and exhibit high participation, effective governance, and a strong political culture. *Flawed democracies* (fifty-seven countries) meet the core criteria on elections, freedom, and civil liberty but are deficient on political participation and culture. *Hybrid regimes* (forty countries) fall short in many ways: they exhibit flawed electoral processes, lack independent judiciaries, impede freedom, suffer from high levels of corruption, or are deficient in other ways.

The remaining fifty-one countries are classed outright as *authoritarian* states. They lack even the basic features of democracy. Elections, if they are held, are not free and fair. Checks on government power are weak or nonexistent, so political repression is common. Individual rights are not secure. The media and other information sources are state-owned or controlled; censorship is the norm. Policies and their implementation are designed to support the regime. Often there are high levels of political corruption and nepotism.

To put the figures in perspective: about half the world's population lives in a full or flawed democracy, and the other half in hybrid or outright authoritarian regimes. When I compare systems as being more or less democratic or authoritarian, I am distinguishing full and flawed democracies from hybrid and especially authoritarian systems. Just what the democracy critics have in mind with their calls for ecological or scientific autocracy is hard to determine, because their definition of the alternative to democracy is usually vague. On the basis of their criticisms, however, it is fair to assume they envision a governance system that would rate either as hybrid or as outright authoritarian.

The top-ranking nations in the Index are mostly small European or British Commonwealth countries. Norway, Iceland, Sweden, New Zealand, Denmark, Canada, Ireland, Switzerland, Finland, and Australia make up the top ten. The high-ranking countries with large populations are Germany (at 13) and the United Kingdom (16), with the US following at 21 (tied with Italy). At the other end of the scale, authoritarian systems include Ethiopia (125), Egypt (133), Russia (134), China (136), Iran (154), Syria (166), and North Korea at 167. India, the second largest country in population and a key actor in global climate action, ranks fairly highly in 32nd place. Table 1.2 lists the characteristics of the four regime types and some leading examples of each.

Can Democracy Handle Climate Change?

Table 1.2: Characteristics of Regime Types with Examples

Regime type	Characteristics	Examples
Full democracies	• Free & fair elections • Respect political freedoms/civil liberties • Satisfactory functioning of government • Political culture for flourishing democracy • Independent & diverse media • Checks & balances on exercise of power • Independent judiciary/rule of law	Norway Sweden New Zealand Germany Canada Australia Uruguay
Flawed democracies	• Free & fair elections • Independent/diverse media • Checks on exercise of power • Respect basic freedoms & liberties • Problems in functioning of government • Low levels of political participation • Less developed/supportive political culture	United States Italy France South Korea India Argentina Mexico
Hybrid regimes	• Elections not free & fair/have irregularities • Government pressure on opposition parties • Weakness in political culture/participation • Weak civil society/high corruption levels • Judiciary lacking in independence • Media harassment/lacks independence • Problems in functioning of government	Ecuador Kenya Turkey Thailand Morocco Nigeria Pakistan
Authoritarian regimes	• Lacking in political pluralism • No elections, or they are not free & fair • Political repression/censorship are common • No independent judiciary • Disregard for/abuses of civil liberties • Media state-owned or controlled • Very weak or nonexistent civil society	Ethiopia Cuba Vietnam Egypt Russia China North Korea

Source: Economist Intelligence Unit's Democracy Index 2016

For democracy advocates, the shift away from democracy registered in 2016 is a worrisome trend. While thirty-eight countries improved over 2015, nearly twice as many (seventy-two) declined. No region of the world improved, and five regressed: Eastern Europe, Latin America, the Middle East and North Africa, Sub-Saharan Africa, and Western Europe. Notably, in 2017, "The US, a standard-bearer of democracy for the world, has become a 'flawed democracy', as popular confidence in the functioning of public institutions has declined."[25] Given these trends and the compelling challenges of climate change, debates about the ability of democracies to handle the issue are timely.

To give an indication of the prevalence of the four regime types and the levels of emissions associated with them, Table 1.3 presents the percentage of total emissions for each type. Non-democracies account for half the emissions, so all regime types need to address the sources.

To be sure, other measures of democracy exist. The research discussed in Chapter 3 relies heavily on the Freedom House and Polity measures developed by political scientists. Some of it also uses the Bertelsmann Transformation Index, which does not assess established democracies. Each has

Can Democracy Handle Climate Change?

Table 1.3: Population and Emissions by Regime Type in EIU
Democracy Index

Regime type	Number of countries	Percentage of countries	Percentage of world population	Percentage of emissions (excluding land use)*	Percentage of emissions (including land use)**
Full democracies	19	11.4	4.5	8.3	7.7
Flawed democracies	57	34.1	44.8	41.2	42.5
Hybrid regimes	40	24.0	18.0	7.8	9.8
Authoritarian regimes	51	30.5	32.7	42.6	40.0
Totals	167	100	100	99.9	100

* The table does not include a small number of countries excluded from
the Democracy Index. This is why the total emissions in this column do not
amount to 100 percent.

** The last two columns list emissions in two common categories: total
emissions excluding those caused or offset by land use and forestry, and total
emissions including land use and forestry.

Source of Emissions Data: CAIT Climate Data Explorer of the World Resources
Institute at http://cait.wri.org

advantages, and the differences in results among
them are not dramatic, but the EIU Index puts more
of a focus on the functioning of government and is
more accessible for our purposes. It also presents
degrees of democratization in useful ways, which
(as we shall see later) matters for climate policy.

The challenge to governance

What does it mean to have *effective* governance? Whether democratic or authoritarian, all governance systems must achieve certain things in order to survive and retain legitimacy. At bottom is the expectation that a governance system will be able to maintain stability and protect its citizens from existential threats. Political stability is a precondition for effective governance; systems that are riven by violence and incapable of establishing order are unlikely to be able to deal with environmental or any other kinds of problems. Similarly, maintaining the territorial integrity and physical security of a country is a prerequisite for successful governance.

Beyond these basics, effective governance means being able to perform a number of other functions. In the economic realm, we expect government to be able to create and maintain the conditions under which people can meet basic material needs – nutrition and housing, for example – as well as higher-order needs such as access to education and healthcare, and economic and gender equity. Historically, the so-called industrial democracies have been more successful in meeting such needs, although recent successes in emerging economies suggest the viability of alternative governance models.

An essay by Stephen Dover from the late 1990s lays out the general case for why climate and other sustainability issues pose novel and complex challenges to governance. Such problems "are different from those in other policy fields, both in kind and degree."[26] The core attributes of sustainability problems include: long time frames; spatial scale (meaning they transcend political boundaries); the reality of limits to human activities, mainly economic and demographic; irreversibility; urgency; connectivity and complexity (in the sense that everything is related to something else); many forms of "pervasive uncertainty"; moral/ethical issues (they are intergenerational and involve critical, often irreplaceable ecosystems); and novelty. Many problems exhibit at least some of these characteristics, yet few outside of the sustainability domain involve so many in combination. Dover concludes that existing governance processes, "which have evolved around problems that do not as commonly display these attributes, can be suspected to have limited ability in coping with problems that do."[27]

Climate change as a policy problem is distinctive for many reasons. To begin with, the effects are not immediate or obvious. Governments have been most successful at responding to problems like air and water pollution, where the effects are apparent and the consequences for health compelling. One cannot touch, feel, or smell climate change, and our understanding of it comes mostly from complex scientific models that reflect a great deal of uncertainty about the rate and magnitude of the change and its effects. As a result, it has been more difficult to establish a political consensus on climate than on more conventional and politically salient environmental problems.

Climate change is also distinctive in that its harm will occur mostly in the future. Getting people to focus on the future when there are so many current issues to worry about is difficult. Humans are hardwired to discount the future and focus on the here and now. As Al Gore writes in *Earth in the Balance*: "The future whispers while the present shouts."[28] Similarly, in his book on the ability of democracies to govern for the future, Jonathan Boston notes that they face a major challenge in making hard choices now about our future well-being; he includes not only environmental issues like climate change but also the financing of infrastructure, investing now in human capital for improved well-being later on, and assuring adequate funding for social security.[29]

Can Democracy Handle Climate Change?

Related to all of this is the perceived mismatch in time of costs to benefits. It is hard to make a case for costly measures now (such as investing in cleaner energy or paying higher fuel bills) for the sake of benefits that may come to fruition later. I stress *perceived* impacts, because many current costs are exaggerated in political debates; there are short-term advantages to climate action as well, such as in energy efficiency, less pollution, less habitat degradation, and more job opportunities. Indeed, it is the shorter-term benefits that may open the way for democracies to act on climate change.

Climate change also poses special challenges due to its scientific and political complexity. Although there is a scientific consensus that global average temperatures are increasing due to human activity and that this will lead to disruptive impacts, many of the specifics are uncertain. We know that sea levels already have risen by an average of 7–8 inches (some 20 centimeters) since 1900, and that half of this increase has occurred since 1993. Models predict that the levels may increase between 3 and 7 feet by 2100.[30] If the Greenland ice sheet melts or other worst-case scenarios pan out, this could go much higher. Clearly, anything at the high end of this range will be far more damaging than a rise at the lower end. The same uncertainty regarding rates and magnitudes extends to most climate change impacts, an uncertainty that enables climate skeptics to raise doubts about climate science and projections, as Naomi Oreskes and Erik Conway portray in *Merchants of Doubt*.[31]

Also among the features that make climate change complex are the ways in which small changes in land and ocean sinks or other factors can trigger abrupt and irreversible impacts. As Will Steffen writes, "the climate system is moving faster than science can understand, and new scientific knowledge is being generated at a rate with which governance is struggling to keep up."[32] Even when political leaders accept the expert consensus it is difficult to keep up with the evidence.

In its political complexity, climate change may rightly be termed the largest collective action problem in history. With collective action problems, many actors must come together in coordinated ways to meet a goal. Such problems cannot be resolved through private markets; they require joint action, often by governments, and typically involve managing or protecting common resources, such as publicly held land, the water supply, and the atmosphere. In the "tragedy of the commons," individual actors with access to the commons consume or degrade it, aiming to maximize their well-being with no regard for the long-term survival of the commons or, in the present case, the effects of greenhouse gas emissions in destabilizing the global climate system.

Climate change thus challenges governance at multiple scales. It requires global collective action, but the form of that action must be determined at national and sub-national levels. At the international scale, agreements like the UNFCCC, Kyoto, and Paris have taken various approaches to engaging national governments in mitigation. At Kyoto national governments were persuaded to make top-down commitments to reduce emissions by some percentage; Paris turned to an alternative strategy of encouraging individually determined contributions to reducing emissions or protecting and restoring sinks.

The primary actors in these agreements were nation-states. Yet local, state-provincial, and regional governance institutions are critical to meeting the climate challenge as well. At these levels, clean energy, climate planning, emission reduction, electrification, and other measures are advancing at a rate exceeding that of many national actors.[33] For the task of climate adaptation – of adjusting to actual or expected climate change and its effects – regional, provincial, and local governments will be on the front lines. Climate impacts will vary depending on many natural, social, and economic factors. An issue to be examined later is whether democracies have advantages in handling climate challenges at a sub-national scale.

Is the critique of democracy all that important?

It may be that the recent criticisms of democracy and its capacity for dealing with the sources of climate change are not that important. To be sure, we do not see mass movements calling for an end to democratic rule for the sake of the climate. If democratic regimes start to collapse it is far more likely to be due to perceptions of economic failure, an immigration crisis, or other issues higher up the political agenda. Most of the criticisms come from the far left and academic circles, or some combination of the two, rather than from mainstream movements.

Yet it is a serious issue that warrants attention. Although climate change in itself is not the top issue on the minds of citizens in many countries, the failure to address it, and the almost certain damages caused by a changing climate globally, mean that it could become one of a range of factors

29

undermining the legitimacy of democratic regimes. What Anthony Giddens terms the "third way" – the pragmatic approach to managing climate change and other complex problems – is being challenged in many parts of the world, as is the role of politicians and scientific expertise.[34]

Authoritarian leaders (and those aspiring to be authoritarian) have gained power through democratic means but then acted to eliminate constraints on their power. Such regimes have shown no willingness to deal with the long-term challenges of climate change. Indeed, in the United States, Donald Trump's populist-fueled administration is the most anti-environmental of the last half-century, totally beholden to fossil fuel interests and hostile to any form of climate action.

There are further risks in putting too much faith in radical, simple-sounding solutions to complex issues, even if they have little or no chance of being adopted. Put simply, they contribute to the growing polarization of political debates and deliver fuel to the opponents of climate action, particularly those in the US who are eager to paint climate activists as pushing for extreme solutions that would undermine democracy and kill economic prosperity. Calling for bigger, centralized government and rule by technocratic elites, as many critics of democracy do, gives climate skeptics ammunition that makes positive action more difficult.

Climate governance is about more than policy – it depends on the ability and willingness to act. Democracy critics calling for authoritarian governance in managing climate change rest their case on our responsibilities to future generations. Consistent with the Brundtland Report, they call for "development that meets the needs of the present without compromising the ability of future generations to meet their own needs."[35] Acting now to avoid the worst effects of climate change many decades or centuries down the road is certainly compatible with that principle. A lack of care now with the climate system will, without doubt, compromise options for the future.

Yet a manageable climate is only part of what we bequest to future generations. We also are passing along systems of governance and everything associated with them. Moving away from democracy in well-established, or what are known as "consolidated" democratic regimes, undermining it in transitional ones, and discouraging or failing to cultivate it in countries struggling to emerge from authoritarian rule – all involve choices made now on behalf of future generations, and compromise our ability to meet their needs. In short, a transition away from democracy toward authoritarianism would be a long-term choice binding on future generations.

Current generations thus have ethical and practical obligations "to consider the democratic no less than the environmental consequences for future people of current reforms."[36] Ludvig Beckman warns us that "the powers taken away from parliaments today are taken away from future parliaments as well," and that "more has to be said in order to make a convincing case for constraining democratic governments."[37] Is it ethical to foreclose options for accountability, fair and free elections, free expression, individual rights, and the other virtues of democracies on the basis of unprovable and arguably unrealistic claims about the virtues of authoritarianism? This does not mean that the deficiencies of democratic and other forms of governance should not be examined and criticized, whether in regard to climate change, social equity, education, or any other issue. It does mean, however, that it is important to make the case for democracy from various perspectives, and to evaluate and respond to its critics, as this book aims to do.

The next chapter takes on the arguments and evidence against democracies as compared to authoritarian regimes. Most of the arguments for the relative superiority of the latter assume an ideal type that is unlikely to exist anywhere in the real world. Furthermore, policy research has found that democracies generally perform better on environmental and climate issues. Chapter 3 explains the sources of variation among democracies in terms of their climate performance. Although nearly all the top leaders in climate action are democracies, democratic regimes may be counted among the laggards as well. The final chapter summarizes the preceding arguments and sets out the case for how democracy can indeed handle climate change.

2

Do Authoritarian Regimes Do Better?

Democracy is a broad concept whose meanings and merits have been debated for a long time. It matters as a normative issue (Do we prefer it over the alternative forms of governance?) and practically (Does it work for handling issues like the sources of climate change?). It is fair to say that, normatively, in most of the world, democracy is seen as something to aspire to. In its more positive forms, it is associated with human dignity, rule by the people, information transparency, political freedoms, economic prosperity, and many other virtues.[1] More practically, democracies have proven themselves able to deliver better outcomes for people in terms of economic prosperity, social and gender equity, and other desirable results. Stable, well-established democratic systems promote economic growth directly or indirectly "through higher human capital, lower inflation, lower political instability, and higher levels of economic freedom."[2] Democracies are less likely to go to war with each other. All of which, of course, opens up paths to a better quality of life.[3] Indeed, as this chapter explains, democracies also manage environmental problems more effectively than do more authoritarian regimes.

Imperfect as they are, democracies have expanded human capabilities and improved people's lives in many ways. Why then do the critics doubt the capacities of democracies, and what evidence exists to support their case? Given the largely favorable impression of democracy, it may be surprising that many critics offer a contrarian perspective when it comes to the question of climate change. The foundation of their view is that climate change poses an existential crisis, as would a major war. If the first responsibility of a political system is to maintain political stability and order, then reducing the sources of a changing climate and avoiding its catastrophic impacts should be an overriding priority. Just as governments may have to restrict liberty and expand their authority in the process of waging war, so too they must adjust to the climate challenge. To quote Lovelock again: surviving climate change "may require, as in war,

35

the suspension of democratic government for the duration of the survival emergency."[4]

The problem is that this will be a perpetual war. Climate change will always be with us. Given its complexity, irreversibility, and its roots in economic structures and processes, it cannot be seen as a problem that will be "solved" over the next several decades, or even within a century. It represents a long-term, permanent challenge to governance. Given this, any departure from democratic values, processes, and institutions in response to the problem would entail not a short-term arrangement but a permanent alteration in governance.

But exactly who are the skeptics doubting democracy and calling for an authoritarian alternative? And what is the case for their criticism of democratic regimes and their advocacy of a different system?

Democracy critics from the 1970s

Recent critics of the ability of democratic systems to handle climate change echo many of the views expressed during the 1970s, in the early days of modern environmentalism. Writers at the time questioned the ability of democratic institutions to deal with air and water pollution, chemical risks, and ecosystem degradation. In reviewing this line of thought, which he calls *survivalism*, John Dryzek identifies two "props" on which these arguments for authoritarianism rest: the need to control access to the commons, and a strong emphasis on scientific expertise.[5] In *Ecology and the Politics of Scarcity*, published in 1977, the political scientist William Ophuls wrote that "we must have political institutions that preserve the common good from destruction by unrestrained human acts."[6] More directly, he asserted that "democracy as we know it cannot conceivably survive."[7] Calling on Herman Daly's vision of a "steady-state" in which economic production and consumption are restricted to what the planet can supply and absorb, Ophuls predicted a politics that would be "more authoritarian and less democratic" and "much more oligarchic" than existing democratic regimes.[8] Reflecting the emphasis on scientific expertise, Ophuls called for a reliance on a class of experts, or what he termed *ecological mandarins*.

In *An Inquiry Into the Human Prospect*, published in 1974, Robert Heilbroner similarly expressed doubts about democratic regimes and institutions confronted with pollution and other environmental problems, arguing it may be necessary to sacrifice freedoms to protect the earth. Given such challenges as ecological harm, nuclear weapons, and runaway population growth, Heilbroner argued, "we must think of alternatives to the present order in terms of a system that will offer a necessary degree of social order" – a system capable of combining "a 'religious' orientation with a 'military' discipline" and thereby offering "the greatest promise of making those enormous transformations needed to reach a new stable socio-economic basis."[9]

In his 1968 essay on "The Tragedy of the Commons," Garrett Hardin proposed limits on the use of the commons through "mutual coercion, mutually agreed upon by the majority of the people affected."[10] Of course, mutually agreed-upon coercion occurs in democratic settings – for example with laws to ensure clean air – so Hardin was not necessarily rejecting democracy per se. On population issues, however, he is unyielding: "The only way we can preserve and nurture other and more precious freedoms is by relinquishing the freedom to breed, and that very soon."[11] It is hard to imagine coercive measures of this form, on the scale proposed, occurring in modern democracies.

Do Authoritarian Regimes Do Better?

More recent critics

A more recent expression of the case against democracy can be found in David Shearman and Joseph Wayne Smith's book *The Climate Challenge and the Failure of Democracy*, which offers a strong critique of the structural weaknesses of democracy – especially the liberal-pluralist model exemplified by the United States – when it comes to undertaking the collective action needed in coming decades. The book makes an extreme case, and it is almost too easy to find flaws, but it illustrates an argument that appears to have some currency.

The authors' perspective is clear enough in the quotation from Aristotle that opens the book: "A democracy is a government in the hands of men of low birth, no property, and vulgar employments."[12] They argue that "authoritarianism is the natural state of humanity, and it may be better to choose our elites rather than have them imposed."[13] They compare climate threats with the struggle for survival in war, arguing that "humanity will have to trade its liberty to live as it wishes in favor of a system where survival is paramount."[14] Like any critically ill patient, the planet must be put "in the hands of a leader, the expert doctor in intensive care, and a team of nurses and scientists, which combines leadership with expert knowledge, decision making, speed, dedication, and compassion."[15]

Although the authors' argument is framed in terms of democracy's general deficiencies, their particular complaint is with *liberal democracy* and its focus on market primacy, human rights, and personal property. As the exemplar of this form of democratic governance, the United States draws a large share of criticism. The close interrelationship of liberal democracy and capitalism is a core issue. Indeed, a stated aim of the book is to "expose the mythical legitimizing role that liberal democracy gives to the capitalist social order."[16] In the authors' view, liberal democracy enables the realization of the worst manifestation of the tragedy of the commons, where individualistic and competitive behavior leads to the ruination of all in the process of ecological degradation.

The solution to the weakness of liberal democracy commingled with capitalism, we learn later, is authoritarian rule by enlightened, scientific elites. But the analysis is thin when it comes to detailing this solution, and the process for the transition from liberal democracy to a vaguely defined ecological authoritarianism is never specified. The authors place great stock in education, replacing money-driven institutions with "the real university" that inculcates scientific literacy, critique of capitalism, and ecological values in its students. Echoing Plato, they "feel that there is some merit in the idea of a ruling elite class of philosopher kings" who can make the hard choices and force the necessary transitions.[17] They offer the standard proposals for limiting growth, reducing corporate power, and asserting ecological over economic values without explaining just how this might be brought about. The only model they suggest is Singapore, which, they argue, reveals the superiority of a "benign authoritarianism" under the guidance of "a team of technocratic elites supported by educational struc-tures" over "the pathetic, self-serving performance of elected representatives in liberal democracies."[18]

A more nuanced view is offered in Mark Beeson's essay "The Coming of Environmental Authoritarianism." Beeson's analysis is less a prescription of what should happen than a prediction of what will occur as governments confront the effects of climate change and other environmental stresses that threaten their economies and societies. Looking beyond just climate to broader environ-mental problems, he writes that the threats to health and ecosystems "may involve a decrease in individual liberty as governments seek to transform environmentally destructive behavior."[19] Referring in particular to environmental conditions in East Asia resulting from its rapid economic growth, Beeson questions "whether democracy can be sustained in the region – or anyplace else for that matter – given the unprecedented and unforgiving nature of the challenges we collectively face."[20]

A response to the critics

Pushing back against the critics of democracy is the sociologist Nico Stehr, a noted scholar on the role of knowledge and science in society. Stehr's particular interest is in the calls for replacing political authority with technical authority – with rule by scientific elites – in responding to the challenges of climate and other complex problems. As he points out, this is not the first time such issues have been raised: "Throughout modern history, one encounters assertions about a withering away of politics and the replacement of the reign of power of men over men with the authority of scientific knowledge."[21] In this view, citizens lack understanding of scientific issues and do not appreciate the effects of long-term trends like a changing climate. This leads many scientists to ask: "Is democracy and are societal institutions that are governed by principles of liberty such as the market place capable of dealing with harms and risks to society that are located in the future?"[22] A related criticism is that democracies "are too cumbersome to avoid climate change; they act neither in a timely fashion nor are they responsive in the necessary comprehensive manner."[23] If the needed change in governance is not adopted, the critics claim, then democracy itself will cease to exist, leading to the obvious paradox that "it is only through the elimination of democracy that democracy can be saved."[24]

Stehr rightly identifies the flaws in these arguments. Problems like climate change cannot be managed by a denial of politics in favor of some form of ecological technocracy. Although Stehr does not address the practical issues of legitimacy and the process of regime change itself – both of which are neglected in the critical writing on democracy – he comes down firmly on the side of democratic governance, its capacities, and the values it embodies. In the end, he asserts, "Only a democratic system can sensitively attend to the conflicts within and among nations and communities, decide between different policies, and generally advance the aspirations of different segments of the population."[25] Technocracy, he warns, is not the solution.

Can Democracy Handle Climate Change?

Table 2.1 outlines the cases for and against the climate capacities of democratic relative to authoritarian systems that are taken up in the remainder of this chapter. There, and in the next chapter, I consider factors that need to be taken into account in evaluating regime types. Among these are the continuity and stability of democracy; the characteristics of interest group interactions; and the specific institutional and other structural (that is, relatively fixed) aspects of governance.

Why democracies should *be better at handling climate change*

There are many reasons why democracies should be able to handle climate change better than the authoritarian alternatives. The capacities of democracies cannot be separated from issues of collective action and environmental problems generally – all involving public goods and common pool resources. Indeed, given Dover's list of the governance challenges posed by sustainability, all of which are present in climate change, this is a problem that will stretch any regime, democratic or otherwise. This is why there is some appeal in imagining a society where decisions are made by

Do Authoritarian Regimes Do Better?

Table 2.1: Summary of the Bases for the Two Ideal Regime Types

Basis for the authoritarian case	Basis for the democratic case
Weaknesses in the democratic ideal type	*Weaknesses in the authoritarian ideal type*
• Cannot overcome status quo interests	• Priority given to ruling elites, not the public
• Voters lack scientific literacy/expertise	• Suppresses information & dissent
• Leaders cater to near-term gratification	• Lacks effective civil society
• Slow, uneven policy implementation	• Uneven global engagement
• Closely linked to neoliberal capitalism	• Undervalues economic/ gender equity
Strengths of the authoritarian ideal type	*Strengths of the democratic ideal type*
• Concentrates authority to force change	• Accountable/responsive to demands
• Centralizes implementation authority	• Quality of governance/less corruption
• Enhances role of scientific expertise	• More active civil society & diversity
• May focus on long-term well-being	• Free flow of information/ expression
• May direct ecological investment	• More engaged in global issues

benign, scientifically literate ecological autocrats for whom the interests of future generations and nature are paramount. Yet such a society does not exist. And in fact the environmental record of authoritarian states is less impressive than that of most democracies, as will be seen later in the chapter. Of course, the ideal democracy doesn't exist either, although some systems are more democratic than others.

There are several arguments supporting the case for why democracies should do better than authoritarian regimes in tackling the largest collective action problem in history.[26] One concerns the ability of democracies to facilitate a free flow of information on problems and their impacts. *Transparency* is the term often used here. Citizens in democracies typically have access to information on pollution trends and conditions, chemical risks, threats to species and land, and other environmental problems. In closed societies where governments control information and freedom of expression citizens have less access to the relevant data. To illustrate the point: awareness of dangerously high levels of air pollution in China grew after 2010 when the US embassy in Beijing began tweeting results from an air quality monitoring station. One expert describes the effects in China and beyond: "It triggered profound change in China's environmental policy, advanced air quality science in some of the world's most polluted cities, and prompted similar efforts in neighboring countries." The embassy data pushed China to create its own monitoring network, revealing "the transformative power of democratized data."[27] Of course, implementation may not change, but China has lately been taking pollution more seriously.[28]

A further argument is that in a democracy people have the opportunity to hold leaders accountable for matters affecting them. The primary mechanism for such accountability is, of course, elections, but others also exist, such as suing government agencies or private firms, waging campaigns against polluters, pressuring elected officials, mobilizing voters with referenda or other initiatives, organizing public protests, and so on.[29] In more repressive regimes such mechanisms are more likely to have been made illegal. But the history of environmental policy is full of cases in which citizens have applied pressure to governments and private firms to make changes.

The capacity to seek, expand, and disseminate scientific information is another strength of democracies. Martin Janicke and Helmut Weidner refer

47

to this as part of a suite of "cognitive capacities" that determine in part the quality of environmental policies in a governance system.[30] Of course, authoritarian societies can have strong scientific capacities as well, but they may not be as good at identifying critical areas for new knowledge, enabling the freedom of research that supports scientific progress, or supporting exchanges with other countries and in global forums. Closely related to this is the capacity for technological and policy innovation. The United States – despite its low ranking, at least among the developed countries, in climate performance – is a global leader in developing and commercializing technologies. These technologies may not always focus on environmental needs, but the capacity is there.

Democracies should also have advantages thanks to their ability to draw upon a wider range of values in policy making. Autocrats typically sustain themselves in power by promoting the interests of narrow elites and drawing upon them for support. They face less pressure to meet public preferences and needs. With public goods like environmental quality, elites insulate themselves by living in select neighborhoods, obtaining higher-quality goods, and securing access to amenities and resources that are unavailable to others. Of course, this opportunity for "privatizing" public goods also exists in democracies, and especially in those with high levels of economic inequality, as will be discussed in Chapter 3.

Since issues like climate change cannot be managed by countries in isolation, democracies also have an advantage in being more disposed to engage in global environmental policy making. They demand collective action not only *within* but *among* nations capable of looking beyond their short-term national interests to their long-term collective well-being. Democracies participate more in international institutions and problem-solving than their authoritarian counterparts. This should be a source of strength.

Do democratic and authoritarian states exhibit different levels of concern for the future? The democracy critics say that the need to respond in some way to citizen demands is a critical flaw: people would rather consume now than save ecological space for the next generation; they are happy to pass along the costs of ecological degradation to later generations. Authoritarian states, the critics claim, can enforce the necessary deferred gratification. That is at least doubtful, and it may be the case that democracies account better for long-term issues.[31]

Can Democracy Handle Climate Change?

Two other claims for democracy are worth noting: that it is better at generating economic and gender equity and that it protects private property more reliably – not just land but financial assets. With respect to economic equity, the argument is that more equal societies are better able to define and achieve shared goals, because high inequality is associated with social distrust. The most direct result of gender equity is the enhanced social and economic status of women, which links with lower birth rates and thus reduces the population pressures accelerating climate change.[32]

Why democracies may not be better at handling climate change

The theoretical case against democracy focuses on its deficiencies in the face of complex environmental problems like climate change, ecosystem protection, and biodiversity. As we have seen, one argument is that in democracies both politicians and voters exhibit what Jonathan Boston terms *presentism*: they "value certain things in the near future much more than the same things in the distant future."[33] This is also a problem because typical voters in democracies are not well versed in scientific and technical issues. Put more bluntly, as some critics do, the democratic public is scientifically illiterate. So, on the first point, voters cannot accept the deferred gratification and near-term costs that come with climate action; on the second point, the case is that they are ill-informed and incapable of grasping the urgency of climate change.

Another common argument is that democracies cannot overcome the political power of interest groups who stand to lose out from climate action. Especially in liberal-pluralist versions of democracy, economic interests are able to block policies such as putting a price on carbon, restructuring tax and investment policies, and transforming energy, agriculture, and transportation systems. To the extent that existing interests have such a power of veto, the path to reducing emissions is stalled. Jonathan Rauch uses the term "demosclerosis" to describe the inability of modern governments to solve problems due to lobbying by vested interests and a "progressive loss of the ability to adapt."[34]

A third argument against democracy is that its guarantees of individual rights and liberty make it difficult for governments to take the needed action. Most democracies are restricted in various ways from taking or limiting the use of private property,

51

regulating advertising in order to cut consumption, controlling the design and use of vehicles, or even taking measures to reduce population growth. Authoritarian leaders do not face these kinds of restrictions. Drawing on the war analogy, it is argued that these are the kind of freedoms that will have to be restricted to allow democracy to survive a changing climate.

In the eyes of the critics, democracies are cumbersome, inefficient, and dominated by special interests. Since they cannot reach agreement on the common good they are helpless in dealing with the complex collective action challenges of environmental degradation and climate change. They cater to the whims and scientific ignorance of voters who are too wrapped up in consuming and exploiting to grasp the threat to the planet and to their own well-being. For the critics, democracies are like a man falling from a tall building and remarking "so far, so good" as he passes each floor. In sum, democracies are *structurally deficient* when it comes to meeting the climate challenge. Even writers inclined to value and preserve democracy can be prone to questioning its capacities on this score. As Dale Jamieson writes: "Sadly, it is not entirely clear that democracy is up to the challenges of climate change."[35]

Do Authoritarian Regimes Do Better?

The evidence on democracy and climate change

The case against democracy being able to handle climate change mitigation and adaptation is based on questionable arguments. The democracy critics seem to envision an idealized, benign, ecological autocracy that places climate action above other social and economic priorities and makes the tough choices that democracies are incapable of making. But what does the evidence tell us? Actual cases of environmental authoritarianism are hard to find. The performance of authoritarian regimes in the Climate Change Performance Index (discussed below) does not inspire confidence, and nearly all top climate performers are rated as democracies in the Democracy Index. A fair amount of social science research exists on how democracies compare to non-democracies in terms of environmental performance generally and in their climate policies specifically. This research does not support the view that authoritarian regimes are better at dealing with climate change.

Although the climate challenge differs from other environmental issues in many ways, there are also similarities in terms of the need to take collective action and to acknowledge the limitations of private markets. Like other environmental problems, climate change involves threats to public health as well as to ecosystems, is marked by high levels of scientific complexity, and requires societies to confront long-term, often irreversible effects. The difference is that climate change involves more of all of these factors – more global collective action, longer time frames, even more scientific and technical complexity. But since the similarities exist, it is worth considering the research generally on environmental performance before moving on to address climate change specifically. That research finds that democracies do better on most environmental problems, especially those that affect health and well-being in direct and visible ways. Many early studies examined air and water pollution. They found that "liberal democracies are more willing to regulate environmental effluents"[36] and that "the degree of democracy has an independent positive effect on air quality."[37]

Among the conclusions coming from these studies is that expanding democracy globally would lead to a better environment. One comprehensive assessment concluded that "a rise in democracy reduces environmental degradation and improves environmental performance."[38] This study looked at five indicators of environmental performance: carbon dioxide and nitrogen dioxide emissions, organics in water, deforestation, and land degradation. It focused specifically on differences between democratic and authoritarian countries and controlled for other factors that affect performance, such as per capita income, openness to trade, population density, and levels of involvement in military conflict.

The strengths of democracy do not just apply to health-related indicators like clean air and water. A study of sixty-six countries across three continents found that democracies achieve a quality of governance which helps them protect forests, leading to the conclusion that "improvements in institutions that empower citizens through enhancement of democracy, strengthening of individual freedoms and civil liberties, and establishing rule of law will ultimately reduce pressure on environmental resources and lead to better conservation of forest land."[39] Another study on this issue found that mature, established democracies were the best performers. Emerging democracies are less able to protect forests than authoritarian states and mature democracies. Democracies in transition have weak governance and a weak civil society; mature democracies have a strong civil society that can offset economic interests. Authoritarian states, by contrast, are able to offset economic interests only through centralized power.[40]

Can Democracy Handle Climate Change?

Some research compares democratic and authoritarian systems in terms of their degree of commitment to international environmental actions and agreements. Here the goal is not to examine actual performance and outcomes but the willingness to commit to collective action on a global scale. It appears that democracies are more committed to such action, leading one author to conclude that "a more democratic world will be a world with stronger environmental commitment."[41] Since democracies tend to be more engaged with the outside world they are more open to undertaking collective action.

Part of the research challenge is to determine why it is that democracies perform better. In a review of democracy-environment studies on Latin America and Europe, Kathryn Hochstetler found that "liberal democracies are more likely to make commitments to policies and institutions intended to protect the environment than are non-democracies."[42] Democracies learn from other democracies when it comes to adopting the necessary policies, and they are less corrupt than authoritarian systems. Indeed, many studies find that corruption, linked as it is to a lower quality of governance, is associated with poor environmental performance.

Some scholars attribute these findings to the history and quality of democracy. What may matter is not the absolute level of democracy but the *democracy stock*, referring to the accumulation and development of democratic institutions over time. One study on this theme concludes that "The more democracy stock a country accumulates, the lower will be its emissions of sulfur and carbon, all else being equal."[43] It is worth noting that this case for democracy stock has also been made in order to explain democracy's role in facilitating economic growth, where "leaders in established democracies may be willing to impose sacrifices over the short term to facilitate a stronger growth performance over the course of their administration."[44]

In the research on environmental protection there is then a lot of support for the argument that democracies are better able to deal with climate change. However, as noted earlier, while climate change is similar to more conventional environmental issues like air and water pollution or hazardous waste, it is also different in fundamental respects. Air and water pollution are more visible and pose near-term threats to health and well-being. Both are more politically salient to people concerned about the effects of such pollution on their health or that of their children. Awareness of climate issues, by contrast, depends on scientific models or on real-world effects that are not clearly linked to causes. Conventional pollution has been managed for the most part with technology fixes that involve minimal economic and social disruption; climate change demands transformative change.

A recent study focusing specifically on climate performance reinforced the importance of a long history of stable democracy. Using an indicator known as the Climate Laws, Institutions, and Measures Index (CLIMI), which looks at policies rather than outcomes, Per Fredriksson and Eric Neumayer found that what they term "democracy capital stock" determines a country's climate policies rather than its current level of democracy. As mentioned earlier, this is "a country's accumu-lated stock of civic and social assets built by historical experience with democracy."[45] A history of democracy raises expectations about continuity and stability, and this "increases the time horizon of politicians and political parties."[46] This longer time horizon not only enhances economic growth, it also discourages industry from trying to delay compliance and supports actions for addressing long-term issues like climate change.[47]

Much of the recent research uses the Climate Change Performance Index (CCPI) as a measure of a country's effectiveness in handling climate change.[48] A project of Germanwatch and Climate

Do Authoritarian Regimes Do Better?

Action Network Europe, the CCPI combines outcome and policy indicators to present a comprehensive picture of a country's climate profile and is updated annually. Emission levels and recent emission trends make up 60 percent of the Index; data on energy efficiency and renewables comprise another 20 percent. The remaining one-fifth of the Index assesses a country's policies based on a survey of some 300 energy and climate experts around the world. This allows not just an evaluation of performance (emissions and renewables) but of policies that affect performance.

Research by Marianne Kneuer has shed light on variations in climate performance among the less established democracies and moderate to hardline authoritarian regimes. She uses the Bertelsmann Transition Index to evaluate five regime types across 129 countries: consolidating democracy (transitional regimes that are at risk of reverting to non-democracy); defective democracy; highly defective democracy; moderate autocracy; and hardline autocracy. Kneuer finds no evidence that hardline autocracies perform any better in the CCPI than do the consolidating democracies. Indeed, "countries representing the capitalist autocratic model like Russia, China, and in some measure Singapore lag far behind the democracies."[49] Nearly all the hardline autocracies were rated as "very poor" in the CCPI. The differences were less clear for the three regime types in the middle, so the quality and strength of a democracy still seems to matter. The core of the democracy advantage lies in the quality of governance. Good governance is "participatory, consensus-oriented, accountable, transparent, responsive, effective and efficient, equitable and inclusive, and in accordance with the rule of law."[50] And as Kneuer adds, "it is reasonable to doubt whether good governance can actually flourish in autocracies."[51]

An interesting 2009 study of climate policy commitments in 185 countries between 1990 and 2004 found that while democracies were more likely to commit to policies for mitigating climate change they were not observably better in actually reducing emissions. They want to do better and are committed to cutting emissions, but they do not necessarily deliver. The positive effects of democracy, the authors found, have "not been able to override the countervailing forces that emanate from the free rider problem, the discounting of future benefits of climate change mitigation, and other factors that cut against efforts to reduce emissions."[52] This, of course, underscores the governance challenge of climate change, even in the more effective democracies.

Do Authoritarian Regimes Do Better?

Also using the CCPI, Frederic Hanusch found that climate policies – and to a lesser extent mitigation performance – are better in democracies, and that "more democratic democracies deal more successfully with climate change."[53] Similarly, in a review of the research, Anna Petherick observes that democracies not only deliver higher incomes, protect human rights, and are less likely to go to war, they also show a greater commitment to mitigation (although still needing better follow-through). Clearly the *quality* of democracy is a critical factor here – the extent to which a regime meets the many criteria for democratic effectiveness. As Petherick notes: "democracy cannot be middling if it is to help the climate."[54]

In sum, democracies will perform better in climate action than non-democracies, and strong ones even more so. But how exactly do democracies differ, and why do some do better than others?

3

Why Democracies Differ

Recall from the last chapter that the CCPI is an annual assessment and ranking of countries in terms of their climate mitigation performance and policies. The 2017 ranking included fifty-eight countries. Although ranked at the top, France was in the fourth spot. As in past years, the first three places were left empty, because "no country has yet done enough to prevent the dangerous impacts of climate change."[1] Of course, the same could be said of any challenge faced by modern governments: none of them are doing enough to reduce poverty, improve children's health and nutrition, protect air quality, reduce crime, enhance economic equity, or meet many other expectations. But what distinguishes climate change from these other challenges is the sense that the clock is ticking and the consequences are profound and irreversible. Adding to the urgency is the evidence suggesting that the rate and magnitude of climate change impacts could meet or exceed our worst-case assumptions.

France's top rating in the CCPI rests in large part on its heavy reliance on nuclear energy to generate electrical power. The origins of this reliance on carbon-free nuclear power lie not in an appreciation of the risks of climate change but with decisions made in the 1970s at the height of the oil embargoes. As Anthony Giddens notes, "France took the decision to become more independent of world energy markets and invested heavily in nuclear power."[2] Having been ranked top in the previous five years, Denmark slipped several spots in 2017 as a result of policy changes being made by a new government. Still, Denmark is a high performer, due in part to intensive use of wind power: it leads the world in the generation of electricity from wind – more than 40 percent at present, with the goal of reaching 50 percent by 2020 – and aims to be entirely free of fossil fuels by 2025.[3]

Consistent with the evidence presented in the previous chapter, it is worth noting that of the top thirty countries in the CCPI (those rated very good, good, or moderate), twenty-eight are considered to be full democracies (thirteen) or flawed democracies (fifteen) in the EIU Index. The other two rated "good" are Morocco (hybrid) and Egypt (authoritarian). Still, among the twenty-eight countries in the lower rankings – rated as poor or very poor – some are also democracies. Among these are the United States, Canada, Australia, and Japan. It may be, as Robert Looney argues, that the case against democracy on climate change is "based less on the actions of democracies as a whole than on the failures of a conspicuous few."[4]

At least at a national level, some democracies exhibit leadership on climate change, while others look more like laggards. It is worth exploring why this is the case, and understanding what factors might account for these differences. As Peter Christoff and Robin Eckersley observe, "there are many different types of democracy, not all of which are equally adept at managing the complex challenges of climate change."[5] Do parliamentary, fusion-of-power systems have any structural advantages over presidential, separation-of-power ones? Are some forms of legislative representation and electoral process more suited to climate problem-solving than others? Do different patterns of governance among democracies matter that much at all? Does the presence of a large and influential fossil fuel industry in a country do more to impede climate action?

Why Democracies Differ

The political scientist Roger Karapin offers a framework for examining sources of variations in climate policy and performance which he has applied to the US system at both the national and state level. He distinguishes *structural* from *political* factors.[6] The former are those relatively fixed features of a political and economic system that are unlikely to change in the near term: institutional features embedded in constitutions, established patterns of governance, and the composition of the economy. Political factors do vary in the short term and include such features as public opinion, electoral outcomes, the quality of leadership, and the balance of political power among interest groups. In this chapter we shall look at each of these factors in turn.

Structural factors

Do institutions matter? This was the question posed in a 1993 book by Kent Weaver and Bert Rockman that compared different versions of democracy in multiple policy areas, including the environment.[7] Although the authors were primarily interested in how parliamentary democracies (such as the United Kingdom) compare to presidential ones (like the

United States), they also considered other institutional features: federalist versus unitary systems, electoral processes, and so on. This question of whether or not institutions matter has drawn attention from researchers in environmental policy ever since.

Most of what is examined in this research reflects structural factors, five of which will be discussed here: the number of veto points, legislative representation and electoral rules, whether a system is federal or unitary, patterns of governance, and the degree of consolidation of democracy.[8] There are also other structural factors that are unlikely to change in the short term. They are affected by but differ from institutional issues. The two to be examined in this chapter are the composition of the economy – specifically its degree of dependence on fossil fuels – and the level of economic inequality.

The number of veto points

By definition, constitutional features are those least likely to change. Although parliamentary systems are often assumed to be nimbler in responding to new policy challenges than presidential systems based on a separation of executive and legislative powers, the evidence is mixed. The capacity to be nimble works both ways: a political system may be able to adapt quickly to new policy challenges, but it could just as easily move back in the opposite direction when leadership changes.

Still, democracies that include multiple "veto points" – those institutions or actors within a system whose agreement is needed on any proposed departure from the status quo – may face challenges in handling climate change. In a study of climate policy making in democracies, Nathan Madden identifies seven such veto points (he calls them veto players): federalism, bicameralism, a presidential system, single-member legislative districts, national initiatives/referenda, judicial review, and pluralism. In systems designed to check the power of any one institution or actor, such as the United States, multiple veto points may impede the system's ability to respond to complex issues like climate change insofar as each veto point "acts as a barrier for policy adoption by increasing the number of actors whose consensus is necessary for policy adoption."[9]

Based on an analysis of twenty-three OECD countries between 1996 and 2010, Madden finds that when there are more veto points, fewer policies are adopted and those that are taken up effect only incremental rather than major changes. This suggests that, institutionally, countries like the United States face challenges on climate mitigation, which of course demands major policy change. The United States exhibits six of Madden's seven veto points, with the exception of national initiatives or referenda. This contrasts with parliamentary systems that have fewer veto points.

Legislative representation and electoral rules

Two sets of structural/institutional factors seem to help a country's environmental and climate performance: having proportional representation in the national legislature with multi-member electoral districts, and being a consensual democracy that integrates competing goals. Countries with proportional representation and multi-member districts (such as Germany) may have an edge over those with winner-take-all, single-member districts (such as the United States). The former have two advantages. First, new or marginal parties representing particular interests have a chance of gaining seats in the legislature and thereby influencing policy. Part of the reason for Germany's strong performance in recent decades is that the Green Party gained representation in parliament and has been part of a governing coalition with major parties.[10] Second, proportional representation creates incentives for politicians to appeal to the middle – to make compromises rather than appeal only to ideological base voters, as happens in the United States. The capacities of more consensual democracies are discussed below in relation to patterns of governance.[11]

Federal compared to more unitary systems

Research on federal systems, like those of Canada or Germany, relative to unitary systems like those of France or Japan offers few clear conclusions. Federalism interacts with other institutional and political features, and it is hard to identify clear trends in the quantitative research. Recent trends suggest that federalism could be an advantage in handling a complex challenge like climate change. The obvious case is the United States, where at the state level some of the most innovative mitigation initiatives in the world are underway, even if nationally, under President Trump, the US has turned its back on the progressive climate policies of the Obama administration.

Another advantage of democracies lies in their pluralism – in the multiple levels of government at which change and innovation may occur. Proponents of authoritarian solutions to climate change emphasize the value of top-down decision making that can force change in the right directions. The complexity of the climate challenge, however, means that no single magic solution exists. Progress will depend on many forms of innovation – in technology, management, policy, and behavior – and vary by political, economic, and institutional setting. A primary strength of democracies is that they create fertile ground for these various forms of innovation.

This strength is strikingly apparent in the United States. While national climate policies have been unstable, varying with changes in political power, many US states have made steady progress on energy efficiency, renewable energy, and other climate-friendly practices.[12] The state of California has been exemplary in this regard. Building on a long history of strong and innovative leadership on air quality issues generally, it has set ambitious targets and adopted a range of innovative policy tools. Its recent targets (all to be achieved by 2030) include an increase in renewable energy production in the state by 50 percent; a cut in petroleum use in vehicles by 50 percent; a doubling of energy efficiency in existing buildings; major reductions in short-lived climate pollutants; and cutting greenhouse emissions from agricultural and forest lands.[13]

Although the United States has not adopted carbon pricing nationally, California initiated a state-wide carbon cap-and-trade program in 2013 and is linking it with Quebec and Ontario in Canada. Nine northeastern and mid-Atlantic states also formed a Regional Greenhouse Gas Initiative in 2009 that not only puts a modest price on carbon but raises funds to support consumer benefit programs for energy efficiency, renewables, and energy bill subsidies for low-income groups.

Most Canadian provinces now have some kind of carbon pricing and climate mitigation program. In 2008, British Columbia adopted what has been called "the purest example of the economist's carbon tax prescription in practice."[14] Starting at $10/ton, it increased each year for four years to level off at $30/ton in 2012. Other provinces have set greenhouse gas reduction targets and adopted carbon pricing mechanisms. To be fair, China has similarly initiated a series of regional cap-and-trade programs, so democracies are not alone in pursuing sub-national carbon pricing.[15]

All of this illustrates the concept of "compensatory federalism" – a situation in which different levels of government compensate for inaction by others in responding to policy challenges.[16] A recurring theme in the research on democracies is that the European Union has strong, positive effects on the stringency of policies. "While the EU lacks important attributes of a fully fledged federal state, it operates as a federal system in the area of environmental regulations."[17] Directives adopted by the EU are binding on member countries, with some room for variation; standards adhered to by the environmental leaders have forced others to upgrade their own policies. EU membership not only promotes harmonization, it stimulates "learning processes" among member nations.[18] In sum, the research on multilevel governance suggests that although federalism is a kind of veto point, in practice it also facilitates climate action by allocating authority across the different levels and units of governance.

Patterns of governance

Among the most consistent findings in the research is that consensus-based democracies with an ability to integrate goals across policy domains exhibit better environmental and climate performance. Some democracies are better at handling environmental and economic goals, which may also influence their ability to handle climate change. In political science, the contrast is between pluralist systems like those of the United States or Australia, and neo-corporatist ones like those of Germany or Sweden. Politics and policy making in pluralist states tend to be more competitive, adversarial, and fragmented.

One study of seventeen industrial democracies found that countries with "strong, centralized interest groups and a more 'consensual' approach to policy making ... have enjoyed better environmental policies than countries where economic groups are less comprehensively organized and policy making is less consensual."[19] Another found that consensus-based, neo-corporatist democracies do better than pluralist ones in achieving long-term collaboration and "positive-sum outcomes" for linking environmental and economic goals.[20] This finding is echoed in several other studies.

In short, consensus-based, integrating democracies have an advantage in identifying and acting on positive-sum relationships among energy, economic, ecological, and health goals. Instead of focusing on the asserted conflicts between, for example, jobs or economic growth and climate action, these democracies are able to link clean energy and other climate action policies with prospects for new careers, market opportunities, and growth options.[21]

Economic composition
Another set of structural factors relates to the composition of the economy. As countries grow economically, they require more energy to

deliver electricity to an affluent population, fuel the production of goods and services, and meet demands for personal and commercial mobility. In the past, these needs were almost always met by using fossil fuels: coal, oil, and natural gas. Countries with the largest fossil fuel resources are often those that are having a hard time cutting their greenhouse gas emissions. Three-fourths of greenhouse gases are linked to the production and consumption of fossil fuels, not to mention other types of ecological degradation. Without a doubt, the ample endowments of fossil fuels in the United States, Australia, and Canada account at least in part for their poor climate performance. Despite its aggressive investment in renewable energy, China (as of 2014) still generated some two-thirds of its electricity from coal plants. India fuels its growth with a similar share of coal-fired plants. Both countries are expected to be high coal users for decades, despite now investing in renewables.

In his study of the American states, Karapin found "much evidence that a large domestic fossil fuel industry adversely affects climate policy, both because the industry is a powerful political force ... and because fossil fuel production reduces the incentives for energy conservation and supply diversification."[22] Clearly then, countries with large fossil fuel resources will use them, while those that lack such resources (e.g. France or Denmark) will seek alternatives. The more fossil fuels are integral to the economy, the more challenging it is to make the transition to renewables. States with fewer fossil fuel resources will tend to have stronger climate policies. Furthermore, political power reflects economic importance: fossil fuel industries have the power to block change, especially in systems full of veto points, where challenging the status quo is already difficult. This is why the growth of wind, solar, beneficial biomass, and other renewable sources is important. Not only is it shifting the balance in energy sources toward cleaner fuels, it will also have the effect at some point of tipping the balance of political power in many democracies away from fossil fuels. Indeed, in states like Iowa, which generated over one-third of its electricity by wind in 2016, the wind power industry has gained political influence and is increasingly able to assert its interests. Economic composition does not change in the near term, but it can over decades.

Economic inequality

Another structural factor that may explain variations in climate performance is economic inequality. Climate affects everyone, but the most harmful impacts will fall upon the poor and vulnerable. The concept of climate justice addresses this inequity, as does environmental justice for ecological and health issues generally. Inequality may work in the other direction as well: we have evidence that high economic inequality undermines trust, and this in turn undermines the ability of societies to take collective action on issues like climate change and other forms of public goods.

To be sure, economic behavior related to inequality may lead to higher greenhouse gas emissions. Inequality creates demands for more growth, including emission-intensive growth, because less income is flowing to lower socio-economic levels. More importantly, high levels of inequality encourage unsustainable consumption levels by linking it with status in society, as captured in the concept of positional goods like big houses, luxury cars, elite schools, and so on.[23] Such goods are valued for what they express about one's status rather than their actual utility.

The more significant effects of inequality may lie in the political realm. Influential economists like Joseph Stiglitz and Robert Reich have made the case that inequality undermines capacities for solving collective action problems, and a great deal of research supports it.[24] In *The Moral Foundations of Trust,* Eric Uslaner reviews a wide range of studies finding that inequities in the distribution of income generate what he calls a "generalized distrust" that increases social distance, fuels perceptions of "us" versus "them," and reduces optimism about the future, all of which affect the capacity of a political system to handle climate change.[25]

Among the conclusions reached in the research is that high-inequality countries spend less on the environment and tend to privilege economic growth over environmental quality. Such countries are also less able to protect forests and biodiversity. Studies have linked income inequality in the United States with higher carbon emissions, and found that equitable growth elsewhere is associated with lower emissions.[26] Low economic inequality in Denmark and Sweden, for example, may be one factor explaining their climate action leadership.

The accumulation or consolidation of democracy
Consolidation refers to political systems with a strong pattern of democratic governance that functions effectively over time.[27] It is a feature of tested and secure democracies, not of transitional ones that may be vulnerable to reverting to more authoritarian regimes and are weaker institutionally. Established democracies tend to

be better at achieving a number of major social goals, including higher economic growth. As one study concludes: "Longer-term democracy leads to stronger economic performance."[28]

Recall from Chapter 2 that democracy is more likely to be associated with strong environmental performance in the long run. Consolidated democracies have stronger political institutions: electoral systems, parties, an independent judiciary, respect for civil liberties, a rich array of interest groups, and so on. They govern with less corruption and have developed a vibrant civil society (e.g. activist groups) able to promote climate action. They are more stable and create expectations of future stability.

Political factors

Unlike structural factors, political factors do change in the short term. In recent years in Denmark, for example, the rise of a more conservative government led the country to fall from first place to thirteenth in the CCPI, due largely to a decline in mitigation policies and commitments. Canada's history as a poor performer will change now that the agenda of Stephen Harper's Conservative Party has been superseded by the more climate-friendly policies of Justin Trudeau and the Liberal Party. And of course, in the United States, the replacement of Barack Obama with Donald Trump dramatically altered the country's climate policies. These abrupt shifts not only impede government progress but send inconsistent signals to investors and others in the private sector.

Political factors include not only electoral outcomes but also trends in public opinion, the state of the economy, the activities of interest groups, and the ways in which issues are framed and contested. Obviously, these all interact with and are affected by structural factors: the institutional rules of the game influence electoral outcomes; access points in the political system shape political strategy; and constitutions define a framework for the relationships between state and federal governments.

Political factors vary over time and among countries and tend to be location-specific. The remainder of this section focuses on two political factors in the United States to explain why it has shown a high degree of climate policy instability and rates poorly in its performance. This may tell us less about the strengths and limitations of democracies generally than about specific aspects of the US policy system and how they are shaped by and interact with political factors. In the following chapter we will consider these factors in comparison with the recent climate performance of China.

Issue framing

Issue framing refers to how issues are defined, debated, and contested in the political sphere. In confronting complex issues especially, people rely on mental maps to organize their thinking about problems, the available information on them, their likely consequences, and possible solutions. Issue framing helps advocates or opponents of policies tell a convincing story.

In the United States, for example, opponents of climate action have consistently framed the climate versus economy debate as a zero-sum situation. In describing the Clean Power Plan, the center-piece of the Obama administration's agenda for cutting emissions and meeting the Paris targets, the Oklahoma Attorney-General and later US Environmental Protection Agency Administrator Scott Pruitt asserted that "What it's going to do is kill our economy, and kill energy production in our country."[29] In direct contrast, the Obama administration had framed the issue by stressing the economic case for the Plan. In 2013, the then EPA Administrator Gina McCarthy stated that

"Responding to climate change is an urgent public health, safety, national security, and environmental imperative that presents an economic challenge and an economic opportunity." It is a "spark for business innovation, job creation, clean energy and broad economic growth."[30] (The evidence, by the way, supports this framing.)

The relative dominance of issue framings varies over time. The seeds for a zero-sum framing in many countries were planted by the financial crisis of 2008 and its after-effects. The perceived costs of climate action shape the degree of support for it, which may vary depending on the state of the economy. In a survey of public opinion, Dennis Chong found that higher unemployment rates reduced the concern for climate change in Europe. Conversely, when unemployment declines, concern goes up.[31] This is consistent with opinion research on environmental issues generally, in which support for protection is higher when the economy is strong. The more climate action and economic vitality are seen as complementary, the more likely support for that action becomes.

Governing philosophy

Another short-term factor that affects climate policy and performance is the governing philosophy that is dominant at any time. In the United States, the national Republican Party has adopted a governing philosophy of individualism, low taxation, small government, and reliance on so-called "unfettered" markets. As Judith Layzer describes it, since the 1970s, "conservative activists have disseminated a compelling antiregulatory storyline to counter the environmentalist narrative, mobilized grass-roots opposition to environmental regulations, and undertaken sophisticated legal challenges to the basis for and implementation of environmental laws."[32] Over time, she adds, this strategy has "imparted a legitimacy to a new antiregulatory rhetoric, one that emphasizes distrust of the federal bureaucracy, admiration for unfettered property rights and markets, skepticism about science, and disdain for environmental advocates."[33] This governing philosophy is antithetical to the national and global action needed to handle climate change. An alliance of this philosophy with the interests of the fossil fuel industries is one of the major reasons for the policy instability and climate weakness at a national level in the United States.

In his discussion of structural/institutional veto points in democracies, Madden also identified two partisan veto points, both of which apply to the United States: divided government for most of the last several decades, and an anti-climate-action party in the form of the national Republican Party, one of the few major political parties globally that ignores climate science and rejects a need to mitigate greenhouse emissions. In short, the historically poor climate performance of the United States may tell us less about democracy and its ability to handle climate change than about particular aspects of current US politics and institutions. Table 3.1 gives a summary of the structural and political factors that have been considered in this chapter.

Lessons on democracy and climate change

The theme of Chapter 2 was that democracies are better at handling climate change than authoritarian regimes. This chapter's theme has been that democracies vary in climate policy and performance, and that long-term structural as well as short-term political factors may explain these variations. For those factors that are hard to change, such as constitutional and other core institutional features, the issue is how to navigate through them in developing a strategy for climate action within democratic systems.

Can Democracy Handle Climate Change?

Table 3.1: Structural and Political Factors Explaining
Variations Among Democracies*

Factor	What the research suggests
Structural/institutional	
Number of veto points	More veto points may impede policy change.
Legislative representation and electoral rules	Proportional representation can facilitate agreement and the positive framing of issues.
Federal or unitary system	The evidence is unclear, but when national action is unlikely sub-national action may precipitate innovation and change.
Patterns of governance	Systems with neo-corporatist and integrating capacities find it easier to reach agreement and to implement policies.
Degree of consolidation	Consolidated democracies have better institutional capacities, expectations of longer time frames, and a richer civil society.
Structural/economic	
Fossil fuel dependence	Reliance on fossil fuels increases transition costs and enables powerful economic interests to block any departure from the status quo.
Economic inequality	High inequality makes collective action difficult, undermines support for public goods, and stresses positional goods.
Political	
Dominant issue framings	Issue framings that emphasize conflicts between climate action and economic well-being (e.g. jobs) impede climate action.
Governing philosophy	An emphasis on minimal government, low public investment, private goods, and "free" markets blocks the needed policy change.

*These are only some of the explanations, but they may account for much of the variation.

Why Democracies Differ

This process will be different for different democracies: the United States is not Sweden, and Sweden is not Mexico. Patterns of governance, often described as patterns of interest-group interaction, are a particularly powerful tool in explaining these variations. Political systems with an ability to frame issues in positive-sum terms are able to reconcile the perceived conflicts between economic and climate goals. They identify and can reach consensus on the positive relationship between climate mitigation policies and the economic goals of steady growth, security, employment, and expanding export markets. In contrast, pluralist systems are too focused on trade-offs, or the politics of the zero-sum, to take advantage of such opportunities.

Economic and social factors also explain variations among democracies. I consider them to be structural, because they are relatively fixed in the near-term, but they are more open to revision than many institutional factors, especially those embedded in constitutions. Dependence on fossil fuels creates a formidable set of barriers to climate action at national and sub-national levels. We see this playing out in the United States, where states like Oklahoma, Texas, West Virginia, Louisiana, Wyoming, and Alaska have led the opposition to Obama-era climate policies. States low in such resources – Massachusetts, Maryland, and California – are climate leaders. This is by no means the only reason for their differences, but it is a factor to be considered.

Since political factors can and do vary in the short term, the key to effective climate action in democracies is to develop coalitions. One path to building a climate action coalition is to frame it as a positive-sum issue that not only reduces emissions and protects/expands carbon sinks but also reduces energy costs, creates employment, promotes global cooperation and stability, and protects health and well-being. Most countries that have moved in the direction of climate action were motivated by worries over energy security, the search for economic opportunities, and a desire for a better quality of life.

In sum, democracies are not all the same in their capacities for climate action. As we have seen, overall, the more established democracies are in the best position to handle complex collective actions like climate change. Their democracy stock leads to stronger institutions and the ability to think in longer time frames. It also appears that transitional democracies are caught in the middle: they lack the action-enforcing capacity of authoritarian regimes, but they have not yet developed a civil society strong enough to counter economic interests. This reinforces the need for established democracies to support consolidation in the newer ones as part of a global climate mitigation strategy.

Without a doubt, city and state/provincial governments will be a critical factor in the ability of democracies to handle climate change in the coming decades. Actions taken in the private sector will be integral as well. Even so, national governments will remain central in determining how well democracies address the problem, for three reasons: they are in the best position to establish an economy-wide price on carbon; they have the resources needed for basic scientific and technology research and development; and they are the primary actors for deciding on and committing to global cooperative action.

Yet there is no reason to conclude that any particular version of democracy is incapable of handling climate change, from either a mitigation or an adaptation perspective. This is not to say that institutional reforms would not improve the abilities of actually existing democracies. Indeed, reforms that enable policy makers to reflect voter preferences, strengthen democratic institutions, or counter the influence of narrow economic interests can help.

One important goal is to strengthen democratic institutions and processes in transitional democracies.

Indeed, this was a conclusion reached in the early research on economic growth, governance, and environmental performance. The main tasks are those of improving governance quality, supporting civil society organizations that promote environmental and climate action, and expanding political freedoms consistent with open flows of information and transparency. Obviously, getting rich countries to deliver financial, technical, and other forms of assistance to transitional democracies will help in improving their governance as well as their capacity for direct climate action.

Of course, deciding whether or not democracies can meet the challenge of climate change depends on what it is deemed to involve. Will it require draconian change in the form of reducing the size of economies, introducing hard controls on population growth, rationing of energy and other resources, constraints on personal freedoms, and government takeover of sectors of the economy, as the democracy critics seem to suggest? Or will it be possible to meet the challenge in more politically acceptable ways? Democracies may be better than authoritarian systems in handling environmental problems generally, but are even they up to the job of dealing with such a complex challenge?

4

How Democracies Can Handle Climate Change

In his essay on "The Coming of Environmental Authoritarianism," Mark Beeson argues that China, an authoritarian regime, "has arguably done more to mitigate environmental problems than any other government on earth."[1] This is because the Chinese government has acted on ideas "abhorred" in democracies. Had it not been for China's one-child policy imposing strict limits on family size, Beeson asserts, some 400 million more people would have been born, adding massively to the environmental stress already caused by the more than seven billion people currently living on the planet.

To be sure, not having 400 million extra people using fossil fuels, needing food, consuming water and energy, generating waste, and converting land to agriculture is a net positive for the earth. Still, the kind of policy adopted by the Chinese is not the only way to limit population growth and its associated planetary pressures. The lowest population growth rates today are in wealthier countries. The history of growth and development tells us that, as incomes grow, the socio-economic status of women improves, people feel less need to have children as a hedge against economic uncertainty, fertility rates decline, and confidence in social safety nets grows.[2] China may have sped up its "demographic transition," leading to lower population growth, but the general pattern is that fertility rates are higher under dictatorships. People experience more uncertainty about the future, because authoritarian regimes are less durable than democracies.

The heart of the case against democracies is that they cannot make the hard choices required to avoid the catastrophic impacts of a hotter planet. Democracies may be capable of incremental change, the critics might concede, but not of the drastic action that must be taken: stopping or even reversing economic growth; dramatically altering lifestyles (less driving, reduced consumption, living in smaller houses); population control; rationing of energy use; forced changes in dietary practices; and so on. But what if such drastic action is unnecessary and the concentration of power occurring in authoritarian regimes is not required? What if democratically acceptable paths exist for controlling and offsetting emissions?

This chapter brings together the case for democracy and climate change in relation to three questions: Is climate action within democracies' reach? What other strengths of democracies (in addition to those examined in Chapter 2) will affect their ability to handle climate mitigation? And, summing up, what are the weaknesses of the authoritarian alternative? The chapter will also look at the ability of democracies to handle adaptation – a topic experts are now starting to address.

What will it take?

Consider what kind of actions will be needed to achieve the Paris goal of 2°C by mid-century.[3] At the heart of any such strategy will be a trans-formation of energy systems through dramatic increases in energy conservation and efficiency and decarbonizing the global economy. In the near term, this means using far less energy and ramping up the rate of renewable energy deployment. In addition, buildings will have to be designed much more efficiently and transport electrified over time. Each of these things is happening now, but not quickly enough to meet the global targets.

Other actions involve changes in land use, forestry, and agriculture. One significant threat to climate stability is the conversion of forest land to farming. This is worse in developing countries where the economic pressures are greater and the quality of governance weaker, but it also occurs elsewhere. Agriculture causes methane emissions (due partly to diets in affluent countries) and disrupts carbon sinks, not only through deforestation but in other ways too, including tillage practices. The climate-enhancing benefits of extensive tree planting – whether in Africa or New York City – may be substantial.

Looking at what it will take to address the mitigation side of climate change (which, of course, ultimately affects how much adaptation will have to occur), the next section considers the results of a recent analysis of the potential for implementing existing solutions. Of course, there is no guarantee that most democracies, or any other regime type, will actually implement them. Still, it is clear that that these solutions exist, and that they are within the reach of high-functioning democracies.

How Democracies Can Handle Climate Change

Project Drawdown

Project Drawdown, led by the sustainability writer and activist Paul Hawken, set out to identify and assess the carbon reduction potential and economic aspects of some 100 solutions for climate mitigation. Drawdown is "the point in time when the concentration of atmospheric greenhouse gases begins to decline on a year-to-year basis."[4] The project analyzed solutions that (1) reduce emissions or create carbon sinks; (2) already exist and could be scaled up to compete as "alternatives to now dominant, high-emitting technologies"; and (3) could be deployed widely by 2050. Based on several data and expert sources, the project calculated for each solution the likely carbon reductions, the net costs of implementation, and the estimated operational costs avoided. The following brief selection from among the top solutions suggests what is possible:[5]

Offshore wind turbines: Performance is increasing; costs are falling. Expanding wind generation from a current 4 percent to 22 percent globally would eliminate 85 billion tons of emissions and yield substantial savings in avoided climate, health, ecological, and energy costs.

93

Can Democracy Handle Climate Change?

Tropical forests: Global forest cover has fallen from 12 percent to 5 percent of landmass. Restoring 435 million acres of tropical forests would sequester more than 60 billion tons of carbon while protecting water and soil quality, adding shade trees, and improving local quality of life.

Solar farms: Rapidly falling costs enable growth in utility-scale photovoltaic solar from the current 0.4 percent to 10 percent of global electricity generation. By displacing fossil fuels this would avoid 40 billion tons in emissions, reduce air pollution, and save trillions in costs.

Educating girls: Overcoming barriers to educating girls reduces family size and population growth and prepares women to be "effective stewards of food, soil, trees, and water," with potentially 60 billion tons of avoided emissions and "incalculable" investment returns.

Several points are worth making here, most of which apply to the list of solutions as a whole. First, the cost savings of these actions exceed, at times by orders of magnitude, their implementation costs. Second, nearly all the proposed solutions yield ecological, economic, social, and/or health as well as climate benefits. Onshore wind and solar panels eliminate many sources of air pollution and ecological damage; forestry initiatives preserve habitat and protect biodiversity, as well as benefit local communities; reducing food waste (also on the list) helps in meeting global nutritional needs; educating girls delivers economic and social returns that, as the analysis finds, are "incalculable."

The Drawdown solutions "are economically viable, proven to reduce greenhouse gas emissions or sequester carbon dioxide, and have the potential to spread throughout the world."[6] As just noted, these solutions already exist. The top eighty on the list would eliminate or offset some 1,050 billion gross metric tons of CO_2-equivalent emissions – enough to achieve the Drawdown goal of a year-to-year decline in the concentration of greenhouse gas concentrations in the atmosphere by 2050. The project also looks at, but does not quantify, solutions that could be used by 2050 but that are still emerging, such as autonomous use vehicles and artificial leaf technologies.

Two recent US analyses of "deep decarbonization" conclude that climate mitigation is challenging but doable. One study finds that "lowering climate risk by building a clean energy economy is technically and economically achievable using commercial or near-commercial technology."[7] The strategy is to move from fossil fuels to electricity wherever possible, shift entirely to zero- and low-carbon electricity generation, and use energy efficiently. An Obama administration report from 2016 similarly stresses energy efficiency, decarbonizing electricity generation with renewables, and low-carbon strategies for buildings, transportation, and industry. It also highlights the role of sinks: "maintaining and enhancing the land carbon sink beyond today's levels could offset up to 45 percent of economy-wide emissions in 2050, with U.S. forests playing a central role."[8]

Democracies can do this

Democracies are better suited to designing and implementing these kinds of changes for three reasons. First, the dynamism and innovation potential of the private sector is more likely to generate the technology and other solutions that will be necessary in the coming decades. Handling climate change will involve more than forcing solutions onto diverse interests and selfish consumers in a society. Second, given that some strategies and solutions will work better than others, or may not work at all, democracies are more likely to exhibit the policy learning capacities essential to implementing the necessary range of policy, investment, and technology options. Third, democracies are more likely to be able to cultivate and promote values like gender equity in addressing the problem of climate change.

So the first point relevant to making a political case for climate action in a democracy is that a wide range of policy, technology, and investment solutions are economically and politically feasible. The second is that climate action delivers ecological, health, economic, and social benefits. Whether conducted under the label of clean energy, sustainable farming, smart urban growth, energy efficiency, green buildings, water efficiency, or any other label, climate action pays off. The key point is that the political case for decarbonizing economies goes well beyond the need for climate action. This is not to say that concerns about the impacts of climate change are not growing: the evidence is all around us in the form of rising sea levels, extreme weather events, wildfires, and changes in ice pack. It is just that worries over a changing climate compete with nearer-term concerns about economic well-being, national security, educational access and quality, and healthcare, among others. Central to handling the challenge in a democracy is the capacity to link climate action to these other social concerns – to emphasize the positive relationships between climate, economic, security, health and other social goals through an effective framing of choices and policy agendas that make such linkages.

In sum, there is a sound and politically feasible case for climate action within democracies. We may handle climate change without disrupting lifestyles, sacrificing core social values, uprooting populations, or upsetting existing economic and political systems. Even contemplating a radical shift from democracy to an authoritarian alternative assumes levels of change that are unwise, risky, counterproductive, impractical, and entirely unnecessary.

Other strengths of democracy

Chapter 2 examined various factors which would suggest that democracies are able to handle climate change, and especially the mitigation side of the issue, better than authoritarian regimes. These factors include the free flow of information on environmental conditions and impacts, often captured under the concept of transparency; mechanisms for holding elected officials accountable; the greater involvement of democracies in global problem-solving;

opportunities to develop and disseminate knowledge that leads to scientific understanding and technology innovation; higher levels of gender and economic equity (at least relative to most autocracies); and a higher quality of governance, in the form of political stability, administrative capacity, low levels of corruption, and the rule of law.

All of these factors are relevant; and most receive support from research. I will now consider other factors that focus specifically on the strategies outlined above.

A dynamic and innovative private sector

In the democracy critics' ideal type of ecological and climate-centered authoritarianism, the tough choices are made at the top and forced downward throughout the economy and society. This presumes, of course, that the choices needing to be made are clear and that successful climate action is largely a matter of seeing that they are carried out on a broad scale. The flaw in this view is that there is no one answer to climate change, either in terms of mitigation or adaptation. Climate mitigation will depend on the scaling-up of technologies like wind and solar and on other technologies that are currently experimental or have not yet been invented. It will require innovation in energy efficiency, conservation agriculture, water treatment and distribution, mobility, land and forestry management, and many other fields. This level of innovation and change is more likely to occur in open, democratic societies with a dynamic private sector.[9] However, the solutions developed in democracies may also be adopted by authoritarian regimes committed to action and having the ability to implement them quickly.

Sub-national leadership and innovation
In countries like the United States and Canada, state/provincial and local governments can keep mitigation and energy innovation alive even through periods of national inaction and policy instability. Climate action advocates increasingly recognize the role these sub-national governments play. Authoritarian regimes are not necessarily less or more federalist, but the concentration of power at the top of these systems removes vital points of access for climate advocates, reduces the opportunities for policy experimentation and learning, and locks the political system into one set of policies. The United States is rightly criticized for being a global laggard on climate mitigation, but its inaction and policy instability at the national level are offset by innovative leadership at state and local

levels, possibly keeping the United States on track for meeting its Paris commitments.[10]

Active global engagement

International leadership on climate action has come from democracies. It is no accident that the major conferences of recent decades were held in cities like Kyoto, Copenhagen, and Paris. Of the twenty-three Conferences of the Parties (COPs) under the 1992 United Nations Framework Convention on Climate Change, nineteen were held in full (7) or flawed (12) democracies as measured by the EIU Democracy Index. Morocco (a hybrid regime) accounted for two of the COPs, Kenya for one (also hybrid), and Qatar was the one authoritarian COP site.

Another example of democratic leadership is the Green Climate Fund.[11] Established at the 2010 COP in Copenhagen, it took on a major role at the 2015 Paris COP in relation to keeping the increase in average temperatures below 2°C by 2050 (with an "ambition" of 1.5°C). The Fund's goal is to raise $100 billion by 2020 to finance mitigation and adaptation in developing countries. Ranked on the basis of per capita funding, all the top twenty countries making commitments to the Fund as of September 2017 were either full (15) or flawed (5) democracies.[12]

The ability to frame choices in positive terms

A more subtle asset for most democracies is their capacity to appeal to voters by highlighting the multiple co-benefits of mitigation. There is ample evidence that shifting from fossil fuels (especially coal) to renewables not only cuts carbon emissions but also reduces health-damaging air pollutants like particulates, protects ecosystems, and conserves water resources. Investing in energy efficiency and renewables also creates more jobs than would an equivalent investment in fossil fuels. Many countries, China included, are investing heavily in renewables in order to expand their export markets. The accompanying box lists some of the top health, economic, and ecological co-benefits of climate mitigation.

Co-benefits that Strengthen the Case for Climate Action*

- Reduces energy costs to business and consumers through higher levels of efficiency in vehicles, buildings, appliances, and industrial processes.
- Reduces emissions of air pollutants that damage health (morbidity) and cause premature deaths (mortality). Among these pollutants are particulates, nitrogen oxides, sulfur dioxide, and mercury.
- Avoids high levels of cooling water withdrawals required to generate power from thermoelectric power generation (fossil fuel plants).

- Avoids adverse habitat impacts of fossil fuel production and use, such as oil spills, surface coal mining (mountaintop removal), pipeline damage, and acid deposition.
- Creates more jobs per unit of investment than fossil fuels due to more labor-intensive employment in the renewables industry, efficiency measures, and infrastructure.
- Develops industry sectors that may attract investment, create export opportunities, and provide paths to the economic revival of local communities.
- Encourages sink-enhancing activities such as reduced deforestation, reforestation, and afforestation that improve air quality; helps protect water quality and soil; and adds to quality of life through the provision of green spaces and amenities, the offsetting of urban heat island effects, and worker productivity.
- Reduces costs over the long time frame of adapting to the impacts of climate change.

*Resources on these co-benefits are provided in the Further Reading section of the book.

This is an area of opportunity in which the more integrating, consensus-based democracies have an advantage. They are better able to identify the many kinds of co-benefits and, more importantly, to agree on and implement policy strategies for realizing them.[13] This may, however, be more of a challenge for adversarial, competitive systems like the United States, with their zero-sum politics and multiple veto points, especially when combined with a powerful domestic fossil fuel industry. Nonetheless, the combination of an innovative private sector, political mobilization across civil society, and effective issue framing based on the co-benefits of climate action may be effective.

What about adaptation?

Much of the impact of climate change already is locked in. The signs are all around us, in the form of rising sea levels, intense storms, declining snowpack, costly droughts, heat waves, and worrisome trends in disease patterns. Climate change no longer is just about the future. Even if greenhouse gas emissions ceased tomorrow, we would still have to cope with serious impacts.

To a large degree, this vulnerability to climate change is beyond a government's control. Physical vulnerability varies depending on geography, topography, water stress, dependence on agriculture, population distributions, and other factors. Resources make a difference: rich countries (those that typically contributed the most to greenhouse gas emissions historically) are in a far better position to adapt than poor ones. They are more likely to be able to build sea walls, expand medical care, prepare for and recover from natural disasters, develop the needed technologies, and afford other measures to enhance climate resiliency.

Political factors and governance capacities also play a role in climate adaptation. Debra Javeline calls adaptation "the most important topic political scientists are not studying."[14] It is more than a technical or financial issue; it also is a matter of good governance. "Adaptation involves protecting our coasts, cities, water supply, food supply, public health, ecosystems, and infrastructure."[15] National or sub-national governments unable to develop strategies, allocate the needed resources, or implement policies effectively will fail to meet the challenge of adaptation.

The University of Notre Dame Adaptation Initiative presents systematic assessments of the climate adaptation capacities of 181 countries. Known as the ND-GAIN Country Index, it "follows a data-driven approach to show which countries are best prepared to deal with global changes brought about by overcrowding, resource constraints and climate disruption."[16] The Index incorporates two components. *Vulnerability* "measures a country's exposure, sensitivity and capacity to adapt to the negative effects of climate change." *Readiness* "measures a country's ability to leverage investments and convert them to adaptation actions." The Index calculates scores for each component to derive an overall score and a ranking for each country.

Nine of the top ten countries are listed as full democracies in the EIU Democracy Index (the exception is Singapore, classed as a flawed democracy, although at the low end). The next twenty are democracies. At the same time, it is worth noting that the twenty-seven top-ranked countries are all placed in the upper tier in per capita income, and the top forty-nine are all upper- or upper-middle-income. Indeed, when adjusted for incomes, the Index reveals a different set of rankings, suggesting that relative wealth or poverty levels in a country are, as might be expected, central to capacities for adaptation. Further research is needed to disentangle the effects of income and regime type, and there are clearly interactions between the two; economic prosperity is associated with stable democracies, and consolidated democracies deliver higher incomes.

The fact that democracies tend to have a better quality of governance may be even more important for adaptation than it is for mitigation. Because there is no body of research on adaptation comparable to that which exists on mitigation, we can only speculate on the prospects for democracies relative to authoritarian regimes in adapting to climate change. A big question is whether its impacts will undermine democracies, especially those still in consolidation, and make it more difficult for others to transition to democracy in the future. Javeline makes a similar point in calling for more political science research and notes that "Many specialists in political conflict predict that climate change and its accompanying drought, food insecurity and stress on state capacity will increase the likelihood of communal violence, ethnic violence, rebellion against the state, internal or civil war, and interstate conflict."[17]

Before concluding, I want to raise two questions regarding the democracy critics: Does their case reveal a lack of understanding of politics? Do their criticisms actually matter?

Do the democracy critics understand politics?

The normative case in favor of democracy is a powerful one, although we have seen that support for democratic values may not be as strong as it once was. Still, it is hard to dismiss the benefits of a system which protects individual rights against arbitrary or discriminatory action by government; which ensures an open flow of information and opinions through freedoms of speech, press, and assembly; and in which people have a say in decisions that affect them, even if only when it comes to choosing their leaders. But set aside for the moment the normative case for democracy: Is what the critics are calling for in the name of climate action at all practical in a political sense?

The most formidable practical issue is the process by which ecological authoritarianism might come about and acquire legitimacy. It seems there are two ways in which this transition could occur. One very unlikely way would be through the violent overthrow of existing democratic regimes. Political systems can of course fall as the result of armed revolution, but it is hard to imagine the conditions under which such violent change in democracies around the world would occur in order to precipitate radical action for the purpose of mitigating climate change. To be sure, many current issues – immigration, mass unemployment, and racial conflict come to mind – tend to promote social unrest and sometimes violent protests. But are any of these issues, let alone conflicts over the need for climate action, likely to provoke a violent overthrow of existing democratic regimes? And even if such a radical change were to occur, what guarantees do we have that reducing greenhouse gases, constructing new transportation and agriculture systems, or accepting low-growth/low-carbon lifestyles would be anywhere near the top of the agenda?

The other way in which democratic regimes can and do become non-democratic is through what Erica Frantz terms *authoritarianization*, where "democratically elected leaders dismantle democratic institutions to seize power."[18] In this pattern, leaders initially gain power legitimately but then "gradually undermine institutional constraints on their rule, marginalize the opposition, and erode civil society."[19] Venezuela is a recent example. From 2000 to 2010, 40 percent of all failed democracies have fitted this pattern. But once again, such authoritarian populism is an unlikely path to climate action: "A robust body of political science research shows that such systems tend to produce the worst outcomes of any type of political regime."[20] They are aggressive, often go to war against democracies, and are unlikely to transition back to democracy themselves.

The question is this: How does a political system that cannot even agree on the need for a carbon tax or for major investments in renewable energy possibly reach a political consensus on the need for climate-friendly rule by a bunch of ecological autocrats? By what mechanisms or strategies would such transformational change even occur? How could the barriers to better climate mitigation suddenly be overcome by way of support for some form of autocratic rule by scientific elites? The answer is that they could not, and the democracy critics are pretending that politics does not exist or can be wished away.

Do the democracy critics matter?

The first chapter raised the question of whether the claims of the critics and their calls for authoritarian alternatives are all that important. Are the worries of scientists and activists frustrated by the slow pace of change all that consequential? They are, for three reasons.

First, they distract us from the challenge of finding real solutions to climate change. Debates about the capacity of democratic societies are worth having, to be sure. The criticisms are certainly worth challenging and disputing, as this book does, and they can inform our choices about the likely paths to a carbon-free future, but they are not the full picture. Second, the criticisms affect political debates, often in unproductive ways. Unchallenged claims about the inadequacy of democracy deliver ammunition to the critics of climate action by reinforcing their assertions about the necessity for a loss of freedom and choice in the battle against climate change. Third, the claims of the democracy critics matter because they take attention away from the need for more achievable, effective institutional reforms and political strategies. The solutions to climate change lie with more responsive, effective, and healthier democracies where coalitions in favor of the necessary policies and economic transformations will be formed.

Furthermore, the critics' arguments could influence foreign policy and the willingness of the developed countries to assist the emerging and poor economies, where the future battle against climate change will largely be determined. It is entirely possible for developing countries to in effect "tunnel through" the Environmental Kuznets Curve – to bypass the necessity of going through a period of dirty growth before confronting pollution.[21] But their ability to do so will depend on economic, technological, and governance support from rich countries.

Can Democracy Handle Climate Change?

In practical terms, the calls for a transition to ecological authoritarianism imply three goals. The first and most obvious is to transform existing democracies into authoritarian systems. The second is to abandon support around the world for emerging or transitional democracies. The third is to anoint existing authoritarian states as climate leaders and aim to expand their influence in global climate action. The first, as discussed earlier, is a high-risk strategy that sacrifices the practical and normative benefits of democracy for some unknown and unpredictable set of alternatives. The second would undermine and impede democratic transitions in countries whose continued political development may better equip them for effective climate action. The third grants legitimacy to authoritarian regimes whose commitment to strong climate action is at best highly uncertain.

Political regimes and climate change

It would going too far to say that democracies *always* perform better than non-democracies or that authoritarianism can *never* handle the mitigation and adaptation challenges of climate change. China may someday lead the world in deploying renewables; Morocco may become a poster child for solar energy; Ethiopia may deliver on its national plan to build an economy based on clean energy.[22] Or at least we can certainly hope that they do, given that authoritarian and hybrid regimes account for some 50 percent of emissions, are major sources of carbon sinks, and in many cases are growing rapidly.

Still, on balance, there is a compelling case to be made on behalf of democracies. They hold too many advantages in terms of being able to make the required choices and supply the needed qualities of governance. They are less corrupt, foster more innovation, respond better to public needs, engage globally, are better at learning across different levels of government and internationally, and encourage longer-term thinking than occurs in authoritarian regimes. Democracies are preferable on so many normative and practical grounds that establishing a case against them is all but impossible.

But to say that democracies have the advantage when it comes to handling climate change does not mean that some are not better, or offer more promise, than others. Some of the differences may be traced to relatively fixed structural factors such as how leaders are selected, how institutions and patterns of governance operate, how conflicts are managed and agreements reached (or not), and to distributions of economic and political power. Others are more the product of variable political factors, such as public opinion, governing philosophy, and the ways in which political, economic, and social issues are framed and contested.[23]

Social and political conditions do constrain the capacity for climate action. Economic inequality may undermine collective action and the valuing of public goods, both of which are critical for climate action. Institutional issues matter – for example voter suppression efforts in the United States that make it harder for minorities and the young to take part in elections. There is evidence that typical non-voters are more likely to support public goods than typical voters.[24]

What of the United States and China? They are the world's two largest economies, the biggest sources of emissions, and the leading examples respectively of democratic and authoritarian governance. Neither is a stellar performer. That mantle would go to small, more consensus-based, high-functioning democracies like Sweden, Norway, or Denmark, or to the sub-national governments of California or British Columbia. China rightly gets credit for ramping up its investments in renewables and leveling off its emissions well ahead of schedule.[25]

114

How Democracies Can Handle Climate Change

The United States is on track to meet its Paris target of a 26–28 percent cut in emissions and is expanding its wind and solar capacities. Neither, however, is setting an inspirational example, and both are justly ranked low in climate performance.

The Trump administration is dismantling much of the Obama climate legacy, intending to leave the Paris Agreement, refusing to pay into the Green Climate Fund, undermining the validity of climate and other environmental science, defunding renewable and clean energy programs, and elevating coal into some kind of cultural icon. None of this, of course, helps make the case for democracy in relation to climate change. Yet there are many ways of looking at what is occurring in the United States. One is that it does not reflect much about democracy as a regime type – it is a product of near-term political trends, reinforced by structural factors (both institutional and economic). In fact, it can be argued that other recent developments in the United States have put the advantages of democracy on display: the vibrancy of state and local responses, the innovation in technology and investment from the private sector, the mobilization of voters and activists concerned about climate change. Indeed, a major strength of democratic governance is that periods of failure nationally may be countered in other ways, through multiple centers of innovation, strong research and technology, and a dynamic investment community.

The path forward

Of course, if emissions continue to grow at current levels and climate change proceeds apace, then transitions to authoritarian governance are highly likely, in many cases inevitable, by the end of this or early in the next century. The widespread instability created by rising sea levels, massive floods, extreme weather, food shortages, and overheated populations could precipitate failures of democracy and transitions to authoritarianism around the world. But such outcomes are avoidable, and the imperative now is to keep them from occurring.

Autocrats feed on chaos. In an analysis of threats to democracy, Erica Frantz notes that "Would-be autocrats can use crisis events to initiate extensive crackdowns on opponents simply by justifying such efforts as being in the interest of national security."[26] It would be deeply unfortunate if climate change were to be used as such an excuse. Exposing future generations to the harms caused by coercive, corrupt, and self-serving governance on the basis of muddled arguments about the inability of democracies to address the causes of climate change is a colossal mistake.

The best way forward is to create better democracies with a capacity for collective action and a commitment to ecological values. The main obstacles all governance systems face, democracies included, are short-term thinking and the power of entrenched interests. Only when societies can look beyond the near term and the power of special interests to their longer-term well-being will they be able to handle complex problems like climate change. The most effective strategy for climate action lies in creating the social, economic, and political conditions in which democracy can flourish, not only for the sake of the planet but to ensure the dignity and welfare of current and future generations.

Further Reading

Climate change poses enormously complex and difficult challenges, and the volume of writing on the topic reflects this. The most authoritative source of information on the causes, impacts, and policy options involved is the Intergovernmental Panel on Climate Change, which is planning to issue its sixth assessment in 2022. Many other government sources also are highly informative, such as the National Climate Assessment of the United States Global Change Research Program, and reports from such organizations as the UN Environment Programme, the Organization for Economic Cooperation and Development, and the World Bank. The Center for Climate and Energy Solutions is strong on the policy options. All have well-developed websites and resources.

An excellent resource on the economic and

social aspects of climate change is *The Oxford Handbook of Climate Change and Society* (Oxford University Press, 2013) edited by John Dryzek, Richard Norgaard, and David Schlosberg. A good source on the global politics of the issue is Anthony Giddens' *The Politics of Climate Change* (Polity Press, 2nd edition, 2011). For readers looking for motivation to join the social movement against climate change, a strong tonic is Naomi Klein's *This Changes Everything: Capitalism vs. the Climate* (Simon & Schuster, 2014). For a more analytical approach to what the worst-case outcomes could entail, see Gernot Wagner and Martin Weitzman, *Climate Shock: The Economic Consequences of a Hotter Planet* (Princeton University Press, 2015).

Because climate science involves high levels of uncertainty and threatens many established interests, a movement to delegitimize it exists, especially in the United States. An essential book on this issue is *Merchants of Doubt*, by Naomi Oreskes and Erik Conway (Bloomsbury Press, 2010). Reading it in combination with Judith Layzer's *Open for Business* (MIT Press, 2012) illuminates the politics of climate opposition in the United States.

There has been a growing interest recently in environmental governance and its role in handling climate change and other ecological and health problems. I devote a great deal of attention to the quality of governance and how it affects problem-solving in *A Good Life on a Finite Earth: The Political Economy of Green Growth* (Oxford University Press, 2018). Two useful books on comparative governance are Andreas Duit (ed.), *State and Environment: The Comparative Study of Environmental Governance* (MIT Press, 2014) and Robert Durant, Daniel Fiorino, and Rosemary O'Leary, *Environmental Governance Reconsidered* (MIT Press, 2nd edition, 2017).

Chapter 4 lists the co-benefits of climate action, and many sources exist for documenting these. On the water-energy-climate nexus, see Michael Webber's *Thirst for Power: Water, Energy, and Human Survival* (Yale University Press, 2016). On the job co-benefits, see the UN Industrial Development Organization's 2015 report on *Global Green Growth*.[1] Moving to clean energy can eliminate health-damaging air pollution, as documented in *The Co-Benefits of Climate Change Mitigation* (Economic Commission for Europe, 2016).[2] On ecosystem co-benefits, see the Union of Concerned Scientists report *Benefits of Renewable Energy Use*.[3] On adapting, see Mark Pelling's *Adaptation to Climate Change: From Resilience to Transformation* (Routledge, 2010).

Further Reading

Climate change involves thinking long-term, a task that does not come easily to democracies or to any other form of governance. For a study of this issue, see Jonathan Boston, *Governing for the Future: Designing Democratic Institutions for a Better Tomorrow* (Emerald, 2017). Finally, on the ways of defining and using concepts to analyze climate change and other issues, see James Meadowcroft and Daniel J. Fiorino, *Conceptual Innovation and Environmental Policy* (MIT Press, 2017).

Notes

Preface

1 Yangyang Xu and Veerabhadran Ramanathan,
  "Well Below 2°C: Mitigation Strategies for Avoiding
  Dangerous to Catastrophic Climate Changes," *PNAS*
  114.39 (September 26, 2017), pp. 10315–23, at
  http://www.pnas.org/content/114/39/10315.full.pdf.
2 WMO Greenhouse Gas Bulletin, 13 (October 30,
  2017), at https://ane4bf-datap1.s3-eu-west-1.
  amazonaws.com/wmocms/s3fs-public/ckeditor/files/
  GHG_Bulletin_13_EN_final_1_1.pdf?LGJNmHpw
  KkEG2Qw4mEQjdm6bWxgWAJHa.
3 Chris Mooney, Juliet Eilperin, and Brady Dennis,
  "Trump Administration Releases Report Finding 'No
  Convincing Alternative Explanation' for Climate
  Change," *Washington Post*, November 3, 2017, at https://
  www.washingtonpost.com/news/energy-environment/
  wp/2017/11/03/trump-administration-releases-report-
  finds-no-convincing-alternative-explanation-for-
  climate-change/?utm_term=.ab40af900b50.

Chapter 1 The Challenge to Governance

1 Leo Hickman, "James Lovelock: Humans Are Too Stupid to Prevent Climate Change," *Guardian*, March 29, 2010, https://www.theguardian.com/science/2010/mar/29/james-lovelock-climate-change.

2 Roberto Stefan Foa and Yascha Mounk, "The Signs of Deconsolidation," *Journal of Democracy* 28.1 (2017), pp. 5–15.

3 See Alex Guillen and Eric Wolff, "5 Big Things Trump is Doing to Reverse Obama's Climate Policies," *Politico*, October 10, 2017, https://www.politico.com/story/2017/10/10/trump-obama-climate-clean-energy-243655.

4 Quoted in Will Steffen, "A Truly Complex and Diabolical Policy Problem," in John S. Dryzek, Richard B. Norgaard, and David Schlosberg (eds), *Oxford Handbook of Climate Change and Society* (Oxford University Press, 2011), p. 21.

5 The IPCC was established by the United Nations Environment Programme and the World Meteorological Organization in 1988 "to provide policy makers with regular assessments of the scientific basis of climate change, its impacts and future risks, and options for adaptation and mitigation." It has issued five climate assessments (the most recent in 2013/14), with a sixth set for 2022. See http://www.ipcc.ch/news_and_events/docs/factsheets/FS_what_ipcc.pdf.

6 Although there is evidence that some top emitters (such as the United States, China, and the European Union) have peaked in their emissions or may be reducing

them somewhat, they are still adding to atmospheric stocks and will need not only to level off but to drastically cut carbon emissions in the coming decades.

7 Intergovernmental Panel on Climate Change (IPCC), *Climate Change 2014: Impacts, Adaptation, and Vulnerability: Summary for Policy Makers* (Fifth Assessment), p. 5.

8 From the November 2017 *Climate Science Special Report*, at https://science2017.globalchange.gov/downloads/CSSR_Executive_Summary.pdf.

9 IPCC, *Climate Change 2014: Mitigation of Climate Change: Summary for Policy Makers* (Fifth Assessment), p. 6.

10 See https://www.epa.gov/ghgemissions/global-greenhouse-gas-emissions-data (sources and percentages); and https://www.epa.gov/ghgemissions/understanding-global-warming-potentials.

11 From the US Energy Information Administration at https://www.eia.gov/todayinenergy/detail.php?id=26252.

12 Available at https://data.worldbank.org/indicator/EN.ATM.CO2E.PC?view=map. These are for carbon dioxide only and do not include the other greenhouse gases. Because gases vary considerably in their warming potential, reports on other gases (such as methane and nitrous oxide) convert them to a CO_2 equivalent.

13 A useful discussion can be found in the US National Climate Assessment section on "Land Use and Land Cover Change," at http://nca2014.globalchange.gov/report/sectors/land-use-and-land-cover-change.

14 IPCC, *Climate Change 2014: Impacts, Adaptation, and Vulnerability*, p. 14.

15 For a detailed review of international activity, see Henrik Selin and Stacy D. VanDeveer, "Global Climate Change Governance: The Long Road to Paris," in Norman J. Vig and Michael E. Kraft (eds), *Environmental Policy: New Directions for the Twenty-First Century*, 9th edition (CQ Press, 2016), pp. 288–310.

16 United Nations Framework Convention on Climate Change, p. 4, at https://unfccc.int/resource/docs/convkp/conveng.pdf.

17 Details on ratification are available from the UNFCCC at http://unfccc.int/paris_agreement/items/9444.php.

18 One journalist saw Paris as "historic, durable and ambitious" and a sign that "compromise works for the planet." Fiona Harvey, "Paris Climate Change Agreement: The World's Greatest Diplomatic Success," *Guardian*, December 14, 2015, at https://www.theguardian.com/environment/2015/dec/13/paris-climate-deal-cop-diplomacy-developing-united-nations.

19 This is according to a Climate Action Tracker analysis of INDCs in October 2015. Other estimates may vary slightly. The point is that Paris alone will not achieve the target, although it builds a basis for further action. See http://climateactiontracker.org/news/224/indcs-lower-projected-warming-to-2.7c-significant-progress-but-still-above-2c-.html.

20 For the United Nations press release, see https://www.unenvironment.org/news-and-stories/press-release/

montreal-protocol-marks-milestone-first-ratification-kigali.

21 IPCC, *Climate Change 2014: Mitigation of Climate Change: Summary for Policy Makers*, p. 4.

22 IPCC, *Climate Change 2014: Impacts, Adaptation, and Vulnerability*, p. 5.

23 Of course, the particulars of variations among democracies may become complicated. The United States, for example, is not a pure democracy but more of a democratic republic or a representative democracy with many checks on majoritarian rule.

24 The Economist Intelligence Unit, Democracy Index 2016, *Revenge of the "Deplorables,"* at http://www.eiu.com/topic/democracy-index.

25 Ibid., p. 3.

26 Stephen R. Dover, "Sustainability: Demands on Policy," *Journal of Public Policy* 16.3 (1997), p. 306.

27 Ibid., p. 312.

28 Al Gore, *Earth in the Balance: Ecology and the Human Spirit* (Plume, 1993).

29 Jonathan Boston, *Governing for the Future: Designing Democratic Institutions for a Better Tomorrow* (Emerald, 2017).

30 Estimates of sea-level rise vary slightly, reflecting the uncertainty, but most are in this range. These estimates are from the November 2017 *Climate Science Special Report* of the US Global Change Research Program, cited above. In a worst-case scenario, this same report concludes, "A rise of as much as eight feet by 2100 cannot be ruled out." This (at 2–3 meters) could put many major cities

under water, including parts of New York and London.

31 Naomi Oreskes and Erik M. Conway, *Merchants of Doubt: How a Handful of Scientists Obscured the Truth on Issues from Tobacco Smoke to Global Warming* (Bloomsbury Press, 2010).

32 Steffen, "A Truly Complex and Diabolical Policy Problem," p. 28.

33 Rachel M. Krause, "Climate Policy Innovation in American Cities," in Yael Wolinsky-Nahmias (ed.), *Changing Climate Politics: U.S. Policies and Civic Action* (CQ Press, 2015), pp. 82–108.

34 Anthony Giddens, *The Third Way: The Renewal of Social Democracy* (Polity Press, 1999).

35 This is now the classic definition of sustainable development, taken from the Brundtland Report by the World Commission on Environment and Development, *Our Common Future* (Oxford University Press, 1987).

36 Ludvig Beckman, "Do Global Climate Change and the Interest of Future Generations Have Implications for Democracy?," *Environmental Politics* 17.4 (2008), p. 611.

37 Ibid., pp. 620 and 621.

Chapter 2 Do Authoritarian Regimes Do Better?

1 For a view on how procedural aspects of democracy relate to well-being, see the United States Agency for International Development's website at https://www.usaid.gov/democracy.

2 Hristos Doucouliagos and Mehmet Ali Ulubaşoğlu, "Democracy and Economic Growth: A Meta-Analysis," *American Journal of Political Science* 52.1 (2008), pp. 61–83. See also John Gerring, Philip Bond, William T. Barndt, and Carola Moreno, "Democracy and Economic Growth: A Historical Perspective," *World Politics* 57 (2005), pp. 323–64. On the benefits of democracy, especially for developing countries, see Morton H. Halperin, Joseph T. Siegle, and Michael M. Weinstein, *The Democracy Advantage: How Democracies Promote Prosperity and Peace* (Council on Foreign Relations/ Routledge, 2004).

3 R. Scott Frey and Ali Al-Roumi, "Political Democracy and the Physical Quality of Life: The Cross-National Evidence," *Social Indicators Research* 47.1 (1999), pp. 73–97; John Gerring, Strom C. Thacker, and Rodrigo Alfaro, "Democracy and Human Development," *Journal of Politics* 74.1 (2012), pp. 1–17.

4 James Lovelock, *The Vanishing Face of Gaia: A Final Warning* (Basic Books, 2009), p. 95.

5 John Dryzek, *The Politics of the Earth*, 3rd edition (Oxford University Press, 2013), pp. 38–9.

6 William Ophuls, *Ecology and the Politics of Scarcity: Prologue to a Political Theory of the Steady State* (W. H. Freeman, 1977), p. 151.

7 Ibid., p. 152.

8 Ibid., p. 163.

9 Robert Heilbroner, *An Inquiry Into the Human Prospect* (W. W. Norton, 1974), pp. 176–7.

10 Garrett Hardin, "The Tragedy of the Commons," reprinted in John S. Dryzek and David Schlosberg (eds), *Debating the Earth: The Environmental Politics Reader* (Oxford University Press, 1998), p. 32.

11 Ibid., p. 33.

12 David Shearman and Joseph Wayne Smith, *The Climate Challenge and the Failure of Democracy* (Praeger, 2007), p. 1.

13 Ibid., xvi.

14 Ibid., p. 4.

15 Ibid., p. 7.

16 Ibid., p. 12.

17 Ibid., p. 141.

18 Ibid., p. 126.

19 Mark Beeson, "The Coming of Environmental Authoritarianism," *Environmental Politics*, 19.2 (2010), p. 276.

20 Ibid., p. 283.

21 Nico Stehr, "An Inconvenient Democracy: Knowledge and Climate Change," *Social Science and Public Policy* 50 (2013), p. 55.

22 Ibid., p. 57.

23 Ibid., p. 58.

24 Ibid., p. 59.

25 "Climate Policy: Democracy Is Not an Inconvenience," *Nature* 525 (2015), p. 450.

26 On the theoretical case for democracy, see Roger Payne, "Freedom and the Environment," *Journal of Democracy* 6 (1995), pp. 41–55; Eric Neumayer, "Do Democracies Exhibit Stronger Environmental

Commitment? A Cross-Country Analysis," *Journal of Peace Research* 39 (2002), pp. 139–64; Margrethe Winslow, "Is Democracy Good for the Environment?," *Journal of Environmental Planning and Management* 48.5 (2005), p. 772; Marianne Kneuer, "Who Is Greener? Climate Action and Political Regimes: Trade-Offs for National and International Actors," *Democratization* 19.5 (2012), p. 867; Per G. Fredriksson and Eric Neumayer, "Democracy and Climate Change Policy: Is History Important?" *Ecological Economics* 95 (2013), pp. 11–19.

27 David Roberts, "Opinion: How the US Embassy Tweeted to Clear Beijing's Air," *Wired*, March 6, 2015, at https://www.wired.com/2015/03/opinion-us-embassy-beijing-tweeted-clear-air. The *New York Times* (January 12, 2013) noted: "The existence of the embassy's machine and the @BeijingAir Twitter feed has been a diplomatic sore point for Chinese officials." See http://www.nytimes.com/2013/01/13/science/earth/beijing-air-pollution-off-the-charts.html.

28 For a review of recent policy see Miranda Schreurs, "Climate Change Politics in an Authoritarian State: The Ambivalent Case of China," in Dryzek et al., *The Oxford Handbook of Climate Change and Society*, pp. 449–63.

29 Democracies may also be more adaptable to changing circumstances. See the brief research review in Kellogg Insight, November 1, 2012, at https://insight.kellogg.northwestern.edu/article/which_government_is_best.

30 Martin Jänicke and Helmut Weidner (eds), *National Environmental Policies: A Comparative Study of Capacity-Building* (Springer, 1997), pp. 1–24. Also see Martin Jänicke, "Democracy as a Condition for Environmental Policy Success: The Importance of Non-Institutional Factors," in William M. Lafferty and James Meadowcroft (eds), *Democracy and the Environment: Problems and Prospects* (Edward Elgar, 1996), pp. 71–85.

31 Regarding "short-termist thinking and myopic policy making," Jonathan Boston writes that "Non-democratic regimes are widely perceived to perform even worse; their intertemporal policy choices often reveal even less concern for the long-term interests of their citizens" (*Governing for the Future*, p. xxvii).

32 *Gender Equity and the Environment: A Guide to UNEP's Work* (United Nations Environment Programme, 2016), at https://www.unpei.org/sites/default/files/Gender_equality_and_the_environment_Guide_to_UNEPs_work-2016.pdf. Also see Jeffrey D. Sachs, *The End of Poverty: Economic Possibilities for Our Time* (Penguin, 2006).

33 Boston, *Governing for the Future*, p. 20.

34 Jonathan Rauch, "Demosclerosis," *National Journal*, September 5, 1995, at http://www.jonathanrauch.com/jrauch_articles/demosclerosis_the_original_article.

35 Dale Jamieson, *Reason in a Dark Time: Why the Struggle Against Climate Change Failed – and What It Means for Our Future* (Oxford University Press, 2014), p. 100.

36 Roger D. Congleton, "Political Institutions and Pollution Control," *Review of Economics and Statistics* 74 (1992), p. 421.

37 Thomas Bernauer and Vally Koubi, "Effects of Political Institutions on Air Quality," *Ecological Economics* 68 (2009), p. 1355.

38 Quan Li and Rafael Reuveny, "Democracy and Environmental Degradation," *International Studies Quarterly* 50 (2006), p. 936.

39 Madhusudan Bhattarai and Michael Hammig, "Institutions and the Environmental Kuznets Curve for Deforestation: A Crosscountry Analysis for Latin America, Africa and Asia," *World Development* 29 (2001), p. 1003.

40 Meilanie Buitenzorgy and Arthur P. J. Mol, "Does Democracy Lead to a Better Environment? Deforestation and the Democratic Transition Peak," *Environmental and Resource Economics* 48.1 (2011), pp. 59–70.

41 Neumayer, "Do Democracies Exhibit Stronger Environmental Commitment?," p. 158.

42 Kathryn Hochstetler, "Democracy and the Environment in Latin America and Eastern Europe," in Paul F. Steinberg and Stacy D. VanDeveer, *Comparative Environmental Politics: Theory, Practice, and Prospects* (MIT Press, 2012), p. 206.

43 Kevin P. Gallagher and Strom C. Thacker, "Democracy, Income, and Environmental Quality," Working paper 164, Political Economy Research Institute, University of Massachusetts, 2008, p. 18.

44 Gerring et al., "Democracy and Economic Growth: A Historical Perspective," p. 332.

45 Fredriksson and Neumayer, "Democracy and Climate Change Policy," p. 11.

46 Ibid., p. 12.

47 The relationship between economic growth and environmental quality is complicated. A field of research focused on what is termed the Environmental Kuznets Curve finds that some forms of pollution decline once growth reaches a certain point, especially in democracies, because the public demands it and the technical and scientific capacity to deal with the problem exists.

48 *Climate Change Performance Index: Results 2017*, at https://germanwatch.org/en/download/16484.pdf.

49 Marianne Kneuer, "Who Is Greener? Climate Action and Political Regimes: Trade-Offs for National and International Actors," *Democratization* 19.5 (2012), p. 871.

50 Ibid., p. 879.

51 Ibid., p. 880.

52 Michèle B. Bättig and Thomas Bernauer, "National Institutions and Global Public Goods: Are Democracies More Cooperative in Climate Change Policy?" *International Organization* 63 (2009), p. 303.

53 Frederic Hanusch, "The Influence of the Quality of Democracy on Reactions to Climate Governance: Why Dealing with Climate Change Means Democratizing Climate Governance." Paper presented at the 2016 Berlin Conference on Global Environmental Change,

p. 42, at http://www.diss.fu-berlin.de/docs/servlets/
MCRFileNodeServlet/FUDOCS_derivate_00000000
6533/060516DemocracyClimate.pdf.

54 Anna Petherick, "Seeking a Fair and Sustainable
Future," *Nature Climate Change* 4 (2014), p. 83.

Chapter 3 Why Democracies Differ

1 *Climate Change Performance Index: Results 2017*,
p. 4.

2 Anthony Giddens, *The Politics of Climate Change*
(Polity, 2009), p. 37.

3 See http://denmark.dk/en/green-living/wind-energy.
On policy changes under the new government,
see Melissa Eddy, "Denmark, a Green Energy
Leader, Slows Pace of Its Spending," *New York
Times*, December 5, 2015, at https://www.nytimes.
com/2015/12/06/world/europe/denmark-a-green-
energy-leader-slows-pace-of-its-spending.html.

4 Robert Looney, "Democracy Is the Answer
to Climate Change," *Foreign Policy*, June 1,
2016, at http://foreignpolicy.com/2016/06/01/
democracy-is-the-answer-to-climate-change.

5 Peter Christoff and Robyn Eckersley, "Comparing
State Responses," in Dryzek et al., *Oxford Handbook
of Climate Change and Society*, p. 439.

6 Roger Karapin, *Political Opportunities for Climate
Policy: California, New York, and the Federal
Government* (Cambridge University Press, 2016).

7 R. Kent Weaver and Bert A. Rockman (eds), *Do
Institutions Matter? Government Capabilities in the*

United States and Abroad (Brookings Institution, 1993).

8 For an analysis, see Daniel J. Fiorino, "Explaining National Environmental Performance: Approaches, Evidence, and Implications," *Policy Sciences* 44.4 (2011), pp. 367–89. This section draws on that review but also cites selected representative research on structural/institutional factors.

9 Nathan J. Madden, "Green Means Stop: Veto Players and Their Impact on Climate-Change Policy Outputs," *Environmental Politics* 23.4 (2014), p. 571.

10 Frank Uekötter, *The Greenest Nation? A New History of German Environmentalism* (MIT Press, 2014); Pers Fredriksson and Daniel Millimet, "Electoral Rules and Environmental Policy," *Economics Letters* 84 (2004), pp. 237–44.

11 An example is Lyle Scruggs, *Sustaining Abundance: Environmental Performance in Industrial Democracies* (Cambridge University Press, 2003).

12 For a recent summary see Barry G. Rabe, "A New Era in States' Climate Policies?," in Yael Wolinsky-Nahmias (ed.), *Changing Climate Politics: U.S. Policies and Civic Action* (CQ Press, 2015), pp. 55–81.

13 These are described on California's Climate Change Portal at http://climatechange.ca.gov.

14 Brian C. Murray and Nicholas Rivers, "British Columbia's Revenue-Neutral Carbon Tax: A Review of the Latest 'Grand Experiment' in Environmental Policy," Nicholas Institute for Environmental

Policy Solutions (Paper 15–04), at https://nicholas institute.duke.edu/sites/default/files/publications/ ni_wp_15-04_full.pdf.

15 For a review, see the World Bank's *State and Trends of Carbon Pricing 2016*, at http://documents. worldbank.org/curated/en/598811476464765822/ pdf/109157-REVISED-PUBLIC-wb-report-2016-complete-161214-cc2015-screen.pdf.

16 Martha Derthick, "Compensatory Federalism," in Barry G. Rabe (ed.), *Greenhouse Governance: Addressing Climate Change in America* (Brookings Institution, 2010), pp. 58–72.

17 R. Daniel Keleman, "Environmental Federalism in the United States and the European Union," in Norman J. Vig and Michael G. Faure (eds), *Green Giants? Environmental Policies of the United States and the European Union* (MIT Press, 2004), p. 113.

18 Duncan Liefferink, Bas Arts, Jelmer Kamstra, and Jeroen Ooijevaar, "Leaders and Laggards in Environmental Policy: A Quantitative Analysis of Domestic Policy Outputs," *Journal of European Public Policy* 16.5 (2009), pp. 677–700. Also see Katharina Holzinger, Christoph Knill, and Thomas Sommerer, "Is There Convergence of National Environmental Policies? An Analysis of Policy Outputs in 24 OECD Countries," *Environmental Politics* 20 (2011), pp. 20–41.

19 Scruggs, *Sustaining Abundance*, p. 123.

20 Mary M. Matthews, "Cleaning Up Their Acts: Shifts of Environmental and Energy Policies in Pluralist and Corporatist States," *Policy Studies Journal* 29.3 (2001), p. 496.

21 This is explored in detail in Daniel J. Fiorino, *A Good Life on a Finite Earth: The Political Economy of Green Growth* (Oxford University Press, 2018).

22 Karapin, *Political Opportunities for Climate Policy*, p. 227. The exception is Norway, with a relatively weak fossil fuel industry and high environmental awareness. Norway ranks first in the EIU Democracy Index 2016.

23 Examined in Fred Hirsch, *Social Limits to Growth* (Harvard University Press, 1976), and Tim Jackson, *Prosperity Without Growth: Economics for a Finite Planet* (Earthscan, 2011).

24 Joseph E. Stiglitz, *The Price of Inequality: How Today's Divided Society Endangers Our Future* (W. W. Norton, 2012); Robert B. Reich, *Aftershock: The Next Economy and America's Future* (Vintage, 2011).

25 Eric Uslaner, *The Moral Foundations of Trust* (Cambridge University Press, 2002).

26 Research on the effects of inequality is examined in Fiorino, *A Good Life on a Finite Earth*, Chapter 5.

27 J. Samuel Valenzuela, "Democratic Consolidation in Post-Transitional Settings: Notion, Process, and Facilitating Conditions," Kellogg Institute, 1990, at https://kellogg.nd.edu/sites/default/files/old_files/documents/150_0.pdf.

28 Gerring et al., "Democracy and Economic Growth: A Historical Perspective," p. 356.

29 At http://www.cnn.com/2016/12/13/politics/kfile-scott-pruitt-climate-change-epa/index.html.

30 At https://archive.epa.gov/epapages/newsroom_archive/

newsreleases/fe40a46647a6007f85257c6200564c15.
html.

31 Dennis Chong, "Exploring Public Conflict and Consensus on the Climate," in Wolinsky-Nahmias (ed.), *Changing Climate Politics*, pp. 110–45.

32 Judith A. Layzer, *Open for Business: Conservatives' Opposition to Environmental Regulation* (MIT Press, 2012), p. 4.

33 Ibid.

Chapter 4 How Democracies Can Handle Climate Change

1 Beeson, "The Coming of Environmental Authoritarianism," p. 289.

2 See Adam Przeworski, Michael E. Alvarez, Jose Antonio Cheibub, and Fernando Limongi, *Democracy and Development: Political Institutions and Well-Being in the World, 1950–1990* (Cambridge University Press, 2000), Chapter 5. For a guide to the long-term climate benefits of educating girls, see Homi Kharas, "Climate Change, Fertility and Girls' Education," Brookings Institution, February 16, 2016, at https://www.brookings.edu/blog/future-development/2016/02/16/climate-change-fertility-and-girls-education.

3 On policy solutions, see IPCC, *Climate Change 2014: Mitigation of Climate Change*.

4 Quotes are from the Drawdown website, at http://www.drawdown.org. The book by Paul Hawken is titled *Drawdown: The Most Comprehensive Plan*

Ever Proposed to Reverse Global Warming (Penguin Books, 2017).

5 Estimates of avoided emissions are based on gross tons of carbon dioxide equivalent (CO2-EQ) and convert all categories of emissions or sinks to equivalent units based on potential for harm. See http://www.drawdown.org/solutions-summary-by-rank.

6 From http://www.drawdown.org.

7 *From Risk to Return: Investing in a Clean Energy Economy* (Risky Business Project, November 2017), at http://riskybusiness.org/fromrisktoreturn.

8 *United States Mid-Century Strategy for Deep Decarbonization*, November 11, 2016, at https://obamawhitehouse.archives.gov/sites/default/files/docs/mid_century_strategy_report-final.pdf.

9 One place to look in comparing capacities for technology innovation is the Global Innovation Index, a product of the World Intellectual Property Organization, Cornell University, and INSEAD. It assesses "the innovative activity that increasingly drives economic growth." Of the twenty-five top-ranked countries, twenty-three are full or flawed democracies. It should also be noted that these are the richer countries, so incomes may explain these results to a large degree, and non-democratic regimes like Kenya and Vietnam are considered to have high future innovation potential. The press release is available at http://www.wipo.int/pressroom/en/articles/2017/article_0006.html#hotspots.

10 On state level policies and innovation, see Karapin, *Political Opportunities for Climate Policy*; Barry G.

Rabe and Christopher P. Borick, "Carbon Taxation and Policy Labeling: Experience from the American States and Canadian Provinces," *Review of Policy Research* 29.3 (2012), pp. 358–82; David Houle, "Climate Policy Resilience in the Canadian Provinces: Carbon Pricing in Quebec and British Columbia," paper presented at the 2016 Annual Conference of the American Political Science Association; Stephen Jones, "Flirting with Climate Change: A Comparative Policy Analysis of Subnational Governments in Canada and Australia," *Journal of Comparative Policy Analysis: Research and Practice* 16.5 (2014), pp. 424–40; Aaron Atteridge et al., "Climate Policy in India: What Shapes International, National and State Policy," *Ambio* 41 (2012), pp. 68–77. A long list of state and local governments, universities, firms, and others formed a "We Are Still In" movement after President Trump's announcement of the Paris withdrawal. See https://www.wearestillin.com/us-action-climate-change-irreversible.

11 For information see http://www.greenclimate.fund/home.

12 Reported in "Status of Pledges and Contributions Made to the Green Climate Fund" (as of September 15, 2017), at https://www.greenclimate.fund/documents/20182/24868/Status_of_Pledges.pdf/eef538d3-2987-4659-8c7c-5566ed6afd19. As of this report, just over 10 percent of the goal had been raised. For an analysis, see Nadja Popovich and Henry Fountain, "What Is the Green Climate Fund and How Much Does the U.S. Actually Pay?," *New York Times*, June 2, 2017, at https://www.

nytimes.com/interactive/2017/06/02/climate/trump-paris-green-climate-fund.html. President Trump has announced that the US will not be meeting the commitments made by his predecessor. The US had delivered on one billion of an original three billion dollar commitment.

13 I make this case in *A Good Life on a Finite Earth*.

14 Debra Javeline, "The Most Important Topic Political Scientists Are Not Studying: Adapting to Climate Change," *Perspectives on Politics* 12.2 (2014), pp. 420–34.

15 Ibid., p. 420.

16 Quotes in this section are drawn from the Index website at http://index.gain.org.

17 Javeline, "The Most Important Question Political Scientists Are Not Studying," p. 428.

18 Erica Frantz, "Democracy Dismantled: Why the Populist Threat Is Real and Serious," *World Politics Review* (March 14, 2017), at http://www.worldpoliticsreview.com/articles/21516/democracy-dismantled-why-the-populist-threat-is-real-and-serious.

19 Andrea Kendall-Taylor and Erica Frantz, "How Democracies Fall Apart: Why Populism is a Pathway to Autocracy," *Foreign Affairs* (December 5, 2016), at https://www.foreignaffairs.com/articles/2016-12-05/how-democracies-fall-apart.

20 Ibid.

21 For a discussion see Mohan Munasinghe, "Is Environmental Degradation an Inevitable Consequence of Economic Growth: Tunneling Through

the Environmental Kuznets Curve," *Ecological Economics* 29 (1999), pp. 89–109.

22 On Ethiopia, see *Ethiopia's Climate-Resilient Green Economy* (Federal Democratic Republic of Ethiopia, 2011), at http://www.undp.org/content/dam/ethiopia/docs/Ethiopia%20CRGE.pdf. Ethiopia is listed as an authoritarian regime and Morocco as a hybrid regime in the Democracy Index.

23 On the role of environmental concepts in issue framing and contestation, see James Meadowcroft and Daniel J. Fiorino, *Conceptual Innovation in Environmental Policy* (MIT Press, 2017).

24 Zoltan Hajnal, Nazita Lajevardi, and Lindsay Nielson, "Voter Identification Laws and the Suppression of Minority Votes," *Journal of Politics* 79.2 (2017), pp. 363–79. On non-voters, see Jan E. Leighley and Jonathan Nagler, *Who Votes Now? Demographics, Issues, Inequality, and Turnout in the United States* (Princeton University Press, 2014). It is no accident that opponents of climate mitigation in the US are also those pushing for strict voter identification laws.

25 On China, see Kelly Sims Gallagher and Joanna I. Lewis, "China's Quest for a Green Economy," in Vig and Kraft (eds), *Environmental Policy*, pp. 333–56.

26 Frantz, "Democracy Dismantled."

Further Reading

1 https://www.unido.org/fileadmin/user_media/Services/PSD/GLOBAL_GREEN_GROWTH_REPORT_vol1_final.pdf.

2 http://www.unece.org/fileadmin/DAM/Sustainable_Development_No._2__Final__Draft_OK_2.pdf.
3 http://www.ucsusa.org/clean-energy/renewable-energy/public-benefits-of-renewable-power#.WgyWf_lSzIU.

www.ingramcontent.com/pod-product-compliance
Lightning Source LLC
Chambersburg PA
CBHW072234250125
20788CB00020B/294